the eco
chick
guide to life

the eco chick guide to life

How to Be Fabulously Green

STARRE VARTAN

St. Martin's Griffin ☙ New York

www.stmartins.com

BOOK DESIGN BY AMANDA DEWEY

Library of Congress Cataloging-in-Publication Data

Vartan, Starre.
  The Eco Chick guide to life : how to be fabulously green / Starre Vartan. — 1st ed.
        p.   cm.
  Includes bibliographical references.
  ISBN-13: 978-0-312-37894-3
  ISBN-10: 0-312-37894-7
  1. Sustainable living.   2. Environmental protection—Citizen participation.   3. Fashion.   I. Title.
  TD171.7.V37 2008
  640—dc22   2008012384

First Edition: August 2008

10 9 8 7 6 5 4 3 2 1

Printed on recycled paper

This book is dedicated to my grandmother,
Doris Ross, the original Eco Chick

Contents

part three ➡ that crazy world
out there

How to Use This Book

This book is not meant to be read front to back; in fact, it doesn't need to be read in any particular order. Open to any section for the information that applies to you and your situation. Are you into fashion? Check out chapter 1. Kind of a homebody who loves to cook? Chapter 8 will nourish your inner foodie. Are you a road-tripper? Zoom over to chapter 11 for coverage of travel-related stuff.

As you read and learn to make more eco-friendly choices, starting with what is most interesting to you, it is inevitable that you'll begin thinking about how you shop, your lifestyle, how many resources you use, the products you consume, and the impact they have on you and the planet. So start wherever you want!

If you want to read this from page one to the end, don't let me dissuade you (and likewise, feel free to start at the end and read backward). But no matter how you use this book, be sure to have fun and enjoy the learning process. You'll find in-depth articles, suggestions, new ideas, and solutions that are modern, old-fashioned, and everything in between, so have an open mind. I suggest resources and products (most of which I've used personally) to help guide your shopping, so keep an eye out for My Green Shopping Basket lists at the end of sections, and check the additional resources at the end of the book. You'll also find lots of new and updated information on the Eco Chick blog (*http://www.eco-chick.com*), so stop by for the latest news and use the search function to find out more about your favorite topics. What you learn will help guide you in making more conscious decisions about your own health and the health of the environment for the rest of your life.

Why You Should Be an Eco Chick

Nobody can ignore the fact that there's an environmental crisis going on. Between wacky weather courtesy of global warming; environmental toxins showing up in our food, water, and, ultimately, our bodies; widespread ecosystem destruction; and the extinction of thousands of plants and animals every year, it seems that all of us are finally getting the message that we are creating some serious problems.

The time to deal with these issues is now, and change starts with each one of us taking action in our own lives. But before you get out the sackcloth and banana-leaf moccasins, understand that just because we are facing a coming crisis with serious repercussions for us and for future generations doesn't mean that we can't still enjoy ourselves, look good, dress well, and even have a great time! That is the mission of the Eco Chick; if we throw a big green fiesta, and invite everyone to come, they'll *want* to make the cool, positive changes that need to be made. If that sounds too good to be true, you'll be (pleasantly) surprised by what you find inside this book.

Being an Eco Chick means doing good while having a good time doing it: it is NOT about depriving yourself, but about rethinking how we live our lives, and living better—more creatively, more passionately, and more consciously. And don't worry, just because it's good for Earth doesn't always mean it will take a chunk out of your paycheck. Plenty of the ideas in this book will actually *save* you money! Eco Chicks not only cultivate exciting and joyful lives for themselves, but they also always have their minds on how their choices are affecting the rest of the world.

Back in the day, all women were Eco Chicks; they couldn't help it, because to survive, one had to be savvy with resources. That meant using, reusing, and re-reusing. Food wasn't wasted, and whatever couldn't be eaten would be recycled as fertilizer. Clothes were made by hand, and tropical fruit was an unheard-of treat (unless you lived in the tropics!). While this may have been a very planet-friendly way to live, it was hard work day in and day out, which led both women and men to figure out ways to make all that toil a little easier.

Fast-forward to today, and we don't have to live the tough lives our ancestors did. But in order to maintain these life-styles, we use huge amounts of energy, depend on adults and children in third-world countries to do the work that we won't (and then pay them poorly for it), and throw a lot of junk into ever-growing landfills. The depressing truth is this: our lifestyles, right now, depend on being wasteful, taking advantage of less-fortunate people, and consuming in a way that cannot be sustained in the future. We are polluting our air and water, using up oil and other nonrenewable resources, destroying everything from five-hundred-year-old forests to five-thousand-year-old ecosystems, and literally living as if there were no tomorrow. We are living at the expense of humanity's—and the planet's—future. The legacy we're leaving behind could be very grim, but we have the power to transform that legacy, from doomy, gloomy desperation to a bright, green future that benefits all life on Earth.

The choice is ours.

Some people say the answer to this problem is going back and living like we did in times past. I don't agree. While living the simple life might be great for some people, I love the modern world I live in, and I expect many other women do as well. Women are now able to run for office, hold top jobs, and travel the world freely, all thanks to the hard work of those smart, tough ladies who came before us. But however much I enjoy being a modern woman, I don't want to hurt people, or the health of the environment. And there's no reason to, as long as you're savvy about what you buy and how you live. Become an Eco Chick and you'll join women who are living wonderfully complicated, fun and fashionable, warp-speed, high-tech lives AND doing it without hurting the planet, other people, or ourselves. Sounds great, doesn't it?

Of *course* you can't just simply walk around with a belief and good intentions and expect the world to change. You have to make changes by taking action. Here's where it gets interesting—and fun! Action could mean modifying your shopping habits, writing to your legislator, changing the type of lightbulbs you use, or exploring new and different ways of getting to work or school. It doesn't mean wearing a sack dress and sitting at home peeling potatoes, giving up style and lifestyle. This book is filled not only with specific ways your choices can contribute to a more environmentally sustainable world, but also with background information so you will know *why* an action is suggested.

I'll even name names and tell you which brands are eco-friendly (and why) to make everyday shopping easier. I've included lots of retail Web sites so you can use the Internet to stock your makeup bag, closet, kitchen cabinet, and more. The Web isn't just a great place to go shopping, though; it's also a fabulous destination to learn more about topics that interest you, so I'll point out the best online resources that will give you the eco point of view. You'll find this same information on the Eco Chick blog (*http://www.eco-chick.com*), so you can start there and click away! Any recommended sites tackle the topics in a fair, evenhanded way and are usually run by nonprofits and nongovernmental organizations that don't take money from corporations or businesses, so they'll fill you in on the real deal.

Making changes can be difficult and complicated, and

doing right by the environment is not always a straightforward proposition. Not everyone agrees on how to solve some problems, but this book will be your guide, showing you the changes you can make (and perhaps even inspiring you to try some new things too). Think of it as your best friend's advice: you take what's valuable and applicable to your life and take a pass on what doesn't work for you. To know what kind of actions to take, you need to be educated. It's all about what you know, so turn the page and learn how you can take better care of yourself and the environment. Welcome to Eco Chick's world!

Why Should You Trust Me?

One of the best lessons my grandmother, who raised me from the age of four, ever taught me when I was growing up was how to be a critical thinker and consumer. After seventy years as an active American woman she told me the truth that we all forget sometimes: people will tell you all sorts of things to sell you stuff (so they can make money), or to try to get power or influence. Just because someone's written a book about something, is on TV, or speaks really loudly at a party (hey, I've done all three!) does not mean you should automatically believe what they tell you.

But this is why you can trust me. I wrote this book because I sincerely care about the future we all share, and I think we are headed for major ecological disaster if we continue with our wasteful, unsustainable, head-in-the-sand ways. To earn my bachelor of science degree I studied biology, geology, and environmental science in college, and took classes in Earth's natural history, basic and advanced biology, climate change, and ecosystems. I've seen the evidence firsthand of humanity's impact on the planet, through my years of environmental reporting for magazines, and more recently my blog. I've spoken to doctors, scientists, nutritionists, politicians, government spokespeople, activists on both sides of debates, and lots and lots of regular folks who see what is happening in their communities, on their farms, or on their ancestral lands. As a trained scientist, I've read the original scientific reports and experiments regarding topics such as environmental toxins, global warming, and species extinction. I don't know everything, but from my decade of experience, I've learned a lot, and I apply a critical lens to everything I check out.

What does it mean to be critical? I ask questions (sometimes ones people don't like to answer); I check to see if what people or companies say is accurate; I follow the money and influence trails to figure out if information is biased and why; and I trust my gut that if something sounds too good to be true, it probably is.

None of the companies' products mentioned in this book gave me any money for endorsement; they are things I think work as well as, or better than, conventional Earth-unfriendly stuff. I've used myself as a natural products guinea pig and have been attempting to live each year more sustainably than the one before. I don't work for any nongreen company or organization, do not have one specific political identity, and frankly don't even hold any particular religious belief. (I think they all have great stuff to teach us.) I'm a citizen of planet Earth and I'm here to leave it better than it was when I was born.

I welcome complaints, corrections, curious questions, and constructive criticism at *starre@eco-chick.com*. I take compliments too!

part one

all about you, baby!

tarting with your body, skin, clothes, and accessories, this section is All About You and how you present yourself to the world. When you look and feel great, you are an inspiration to yourself and the world. You don't have to adhere to any particular style, but you can enhance your own by making planet-friendly choices. It doesn't matter if you are a clean-scrubbed gardening girl, a night-on-the-town party-hearty lady, a global nomad never knowing where you'll sleep, or a hardworking chickie who has just minutes a day to get going; you'll find great information in this section.

The changes you make, starting with what you wash with, to the kind of makeup you use, to your clothing and accessory choices, all have a significant impact that includes, but is not limited to: maintaining the health of our water supplies, making sure third-world workers make a living wage, maintaining the integrity of topsoil on farms, keeping pollution out of the air, and keeping our own body healthy. So read on to learn how your choices about what to wear and how to smell great (!) impact more than just your look.

One

Super Natural You

Okay, let's be honest, we all have parts of ourselves that we don't like, whether it's a hair-trigger temper or funky toes. Pick your favorite actress, super-successful businesswoman, haute couture model, or Olympic athlete, and ask them what they don't like about themselves; I guarantee their list will be as long as yours. No matter how great they look in photographs, everyone has insecurities, and companies take advantage of those feelings to sell you products—stuff you don't need, and stuff you don't even want that inevitably ends up in the back of your closet. What else besides insecurity explains why we buy things as uniformly hideous as butt-crack-bearing jeans?

The first step in becoming an Eco Chick is relishing the positive aspects of yourself and enhancing them. It's called *natural beauty,* and the great thing is that everyone has it. Your job is to find yours. Do you have luscious locks? Great skin? A killer sense of humor? Legs up to there? A practically photographic memory? Finding what is fabulous about yourself and concentrating on those qualities will take you further in life than subjecting yourself to constant self-criticism. That's the secret all successful people share. Do you think Jane Goodall, the famous chimpanzee researcher who was featured in *Vogue*, beats herself up because she doesn't have big boobs? Can you imagine Wangari Maathai, who won the Nobel Peace Prize for her African tree-planting initiative, getting down because her hair isn't perfect? No way. Yet both of these women have been lauded not only for their great work, but also for their unique style and natural beauty.

What does all of this have to do with the environment, you might ask? The answer is: everything. How you feel about yourself dictates how you treat the world around you. Do people who really care about themselves and Earth smoke cigarettes and then throw the butts on the ground? Think about it. Is a woman who's happy with herself going to have a corner of her closet dedicated to outfits she's only worn once?

Knowing your natural beauty means supporting it, with healthy choices about what you put in your body, on your skin, and what kind of environment you choose to live in every day. Your body is the link between you and the rest of the great green planet. That's why 99 percent of the time the choice that's better for the environment is a better choice for your health too. So start making your list. What do you *love* about yourself?

Whatever it is, put your energies and attention into what's great about yourself, and you may be surprised at how this affects other areas of your life. While you can't change your genes, you can change what you put on your hair and in your body.

Getting Clean in a Dirty World

Personal care products like shampoo, conditioner, bath bubbles and shower washes, facial cleansers, foot scrub, moisturizers, perfumes, and body powders are marketed mostly on how their containers look instead of what's actually inside. No matter how cute the packaging though, what's inside can be downright toxic, both for you and the environment. So you have to do some homework first.

Keep in mind that most labels on shampoos, soaps, and such, including terms such as "natural," "eco," or "herbal," don't mean a thing; companies are allowed to use these words however they want. This includes shampoos that promise thicker hair or moisturizers that claim to retard hair growth, by the way. The organic label is monitored by the U.S. Department of Agriculture (USDA), but is only applicable to personal care products if their ingredients are more than 95 percent certified organic (which is really tough to do when you need to keep something on a shelf for a while, so there are few products like this available). Labels with "70 percent organic" or "85 percent organic" are designations claimed by the companies selling the product and are not the result of the USDA's oversight.

Even those products labeled as containing organic ingredients can have stuff in them you'd rather avoid. The Food and Drug Administration (FDA) only loosely monitors the hundreds of ingredients we wash ourselves with, and there is no third-party or independent testing of products—"natural" or otherwise. Most people wrongly assume that the FDA checks all the ingredients in the things we use on our bodies and in our homes, but that's not the case. There's this list of chemicals, called GRAS (which stands for generally recognized as safe). All those multisyllabic substances in your shampoo are on this list. But being on the GRAS list only means that so far nobody has proven that the ingredient causes harm to people. It *doesn't* mean that it has undergone any kind of testing on humans or for its environmental impact. Kinda disturbing, huh?

Your best defense is education (isn't it always?). See which ingredients are used in your shampoo/body wash/moisturizer. Some compounds you may want to avoid include parabens (they can have the prefixes methyl-, propyl-, or butyl-), which have been linked to elevated estrogen levels and breast cancer in some studies; urea preservatives, which can cause skin irritation; diethanolamine (DEA), which has been linked to cancer in animal studies; and artificial colors and fragrances, which have also been linked to cancer, skin irritation, and respiratory difficulties. Some people choose to avoid sodium laureth or lauryl sulfate, but there haven't been any scientific studies proving that it is harmful, and it is found in some mainstream natural products. (However, it's easy to avoid if you want to.) Most of the other ingredients mentioned above aren't found at all in widely available brands with a serious commitment to health and the environment (see page 11).

As for the environment, just remember that all that great-smelling goopy deliciousness you use in the shower runs down the drain and into the water supply. If you live in a city or suburb, that water is just minimally treated (to kill bacteria and remove large particles), but not purified before it is dumped into our waterways. So all those colors, preservatives, suds, and chemicals go right into our bodies of water. This affects not only us but also the plants, fish, and other animals that live in our shared waters.

The water you use in your shower eventually becomes part of some animal's home waters (and goes into the drinking-water supply!). It's not just your waste that pollutes. Multiply all the chemicals that people in your town use in the bathroom every day, and think of all that stuff mixing together and being dumped into your favorite river, stream, or nearby bay or ocean. Those persistent chemicals come right back to you when you eat the fish that has lived in that water. Because freshwater makes up just 2.5 percent of the water on Earth (and two-thirds of that is locked up in glaciers), it's just plain silly to muck it up with unnecessary colors, fragrances, and nonbiodegradable chemicals. Especially since there are tons of awesome, all-natural alternatives.

Check out Ingredients to Avoid on the next page and search out all-natural soaps that come in bars (less packaging) rather than shower gels, which come in plastic containers. You can find these even in most grocery stores; look for glycerin-based soaps with few additional ingredients. Organic shea and cocoa butters are super-rich, completely natural nut-based moisturizers that can be used on their own or combined with other ingredients, and organic sesame, sweet almond, and olive oils also work wonders for dry skin. There is no need for chemicals in your moisturizers (unless you are told to use them by a doctor), so look for ingredients that are made from substances whose names you can understand, and always choose organic when you have the option.

ECO QUICKIE.

Find out what's in your favorite shampoo, makeup, or moisturizer at the Environmental Working Group's Skin Deep site, http://www.cosmeticsdatabase.com

CHEMICAL SOUP:
INGREDIENTS TO AVOID

Fragrance: The FDA allows companies (due to a loophole to protect "trade secrets") to use any chemical if it's part of the fragrance profile of the product—and they do, including known carcinogens and substances that disrupt hormones. Organic products may list "fragrance" on their packaging, but they use natural plant and flower extracts to scent products, not chemicals.

Mercury: Listed as thimerosol; there are no safe levels of mercury for women of child-bearing age according to the FDA.

Parabens: A group of compounds the toxicity of which depends on the type. Sodium methylparaben and paraben are the two worst of the worst, but all parabens are worth avoiding if you can.

Petrolatum, petroleum distillates: These are petroleum products and come, originally, from the same nonrenewable oil wells as the gas in our cars. Impurities in oil are known carcinogens, and using these products also increases our dependence on fossil fuels.

Phthalates: Plastisizers that are in a huge range of products, from shampoos and lotions to plastic containers. They're toxic enough (causing reproductive harm and cancer) to have been outlawed for kids' products in the European Union, and California has followed suit, starting in 2009.

Sodium lauryl and laureth sulfates: These compounds, which are cleansers, are used by some natural products companies because their toxicity is considered low by consumer's rights groups (though they have been linked to some health issues).

Modified Navy Showers; Not Just for Sailors . . .

If you're a member of the half-an-hour-shower club, it's time to reform your ways. Not only are you wasting freshwater resources, but also heating all that water, only to have most of it go down the drain unused, is a serious money waster. Even if you don't pay your own gas, oil, or electric bill, you're contributing to increased levels of CO_2 and air pollution every time you stand in the shower longer than necessary.

If you're like me, ladies (and I pray you're not, because I'm a hairy beast), you might need to shave your legs every time you shower. It takes me almost five minutes to do both my legs, usually with the water running down my back. It was suggested to me that I try the Navy shower, a protocol the U.S. Navy uses on ships and submarines, which have limited supplies of freshwater.

The Navy shower involves turning on the shower only when you need the water running, so you jump in the shower and get wet, then turn off the water while you soap up and suds your hair. The water goes back on to rinse, and you use half or less the amount of water you might otherwise. I thought this might work for some, but I multitask in the shower anyway, so turning the water off here just means I have to turn it back on again to condition. So my version of the "Navy shower" is now showering as usual, then turning the water off when I shave my legs, which is when I really waste water, and then rinsing off. I don't feel as rushed while shaving, thinking about all the water I am wasting, and I get a better shave, because it's not so foggy while I'm doing it. I also use this time to condition my hair.

Turning the shower off for five to six minutes even just three times a week might not seem like a big deal, but it means you save roughly 360 gallons of water a month, or about 4,400 gallons a year! And not only are you saving water, but you're also saving money, because that water would be heated, costing you cash and using dwindling fossil fuel resources.

Of course, installing a low-flow showerhead (easy to do yourself and available at any hardware or home goods store) will help you cut down almost 50 percent of your water usage, though many homes and apartment buildings already have these installed. An easy way to check if you already have one is to put a two-quart saucepan in the shower, aim the shower head into the middle of the pot, turn on the water, and count how many seconds it takes to fill. If it takes fewer than twelve seconds, you should use a low-flow showerhead instead. If there is a notation on your showerhead that says "2.5 gpm," or a lower number, it's already a water-saving device.

ECO QUICKIE.
Even though the Earth is two-thirds covered in water, less than 1 percent of that water is fresh, clean, and drinkable.

Hair Color for Natural Divas

There are many natural options to the hair dyes you find in that long aisle in the drugstore. A report in the *Journal of the National Cancer Institute* linked long-term use of dark-colored hair dyes with increased risk of non-Hodgkin's lymphoma and multiple myeloma. If you are into reds or browns, consider henna, which has been used for thousands of years by women in India and Africa for semipermanent dyeing of both the skin and hair. Made from the lawsonia plant, henna won't lighten hair, but it will deposit gorgeous rich tones, from bright cherry to auburn, to coffee and dark mahogany. Many hennas come with conditioners mixed in (my favorite henna is from LUSH; they combine the color with cocoa butter), so look for conditioning henna, or add olive oil or avocado to the henna, when you're mixing it up.

Another option for semipermanent treatment is a color conditioner, which you use in the shower like a regular conditioner, or leave on for a while (like a deep conditioning treatment) before washing off. Aveda makes a whole line of these conditioners, and they work beautifully for adding color and shine to brunettes and redheads.

If you want to lighten or highlight your hair, or dye it permanently, you will have to use peroxide. That's just the way it is. But you can find formulations that have far fewer chemicals in them. Keep an eye out and avoid regular use of *p*-Phenylenediamine (PPD) or diaminobenzene; these are the chemicals that are considered the most toxic.

Lastly, if you get your hair dyed by a colorist, talk to him or her about either bringing your own dyes or henna in for them to use, or asking whether the salon would order from a company like Aveda or John Masters, which make professional lines. You can remind the stylist that these dyes are better for them too! A 2001 study in the *International Journal of Cancer* found that hair colorists have higher levels of bladder cancer than the general public. The bonus to natural hair dyes is that your hair will never smell like chemicals!

Hair Be Gone! Shaving vs. Waxing

I've tried it all—home waxing, professional waxing, shaving, even letting my natural body hair grow. (I'm not a fan of that, personally, though *au naturelle* is definitely the most eco-friendly way to go!) Home waxing kits seem to be the most wasteful system of the bunch, with tubs and rollers of wax, weird plasticky stripping pieces, and way too much packaging. Going to a salon can be pricey, and there is the time and driving to consider, though this can be a good choice if you walk or take public transportation, and since the wax containers are reused, it cuts down on the waste factor.

Shaving at home can be a great choice if you turn the water off while you do it (see Navy showers, page 12) and if you use a natural shave gel. (Definitely skip any shaving foam that comes in a huge, unrecyclable metal container; hand-lathered shave gel, or a really rich soap will work just as well). It's your choice! Shaving oils are a new, nonsudsy way to moisturize while you shave, and a little oil goes a long way, meaning less packaging.

Although body hair removal seems like a pretty small thing, think of a lifetime's worth of disposable razors stacked up alongside all their packaging, next to thousands of shave gel containers. Keeping all of that from ending up in landfills (not to mention the oil, gas, and other limited resources used to manufacture, create, and ship these products to begin with) is a really good example of how making a small change can have a significant impact on the waste you produce.

eco chick essential

If you use disposable razors, stop right now! Invest in a razor in which *only* the blades need replacing. If you must use disposable razors for some reason, there are recycled and recyclable versions available; my favorites are from Recycline. The best natural shaving cream to get silky smooth with? Hands down it's Kiss My Face's, which comes in a variety of scents.

Why You Should Care About Your Lube

The only time I really like to think about lube is when I'm buying it, and even then I have to admit I haven't scrutinized the ingredients as I would if I were picking up a moisturizer or shampoo. But for the same reasons it's best to opt for natural ingredients in makeup and bath products (you're absorbing some into your body every time you use the stuff), you want to consider a lube with fewer chemical constituents.

Most lubes have one of three bases: water, silicone, or oil. Water-based lubes are the most popular, since you can use them safely with condoms. Unfortunately, most common water-based lubes contain a panoply of chemicals besides water, including parabens—which the Breast Cancer Fund has recently identified as possibly causing cancer—and propylene and polyethelene glycols, which are petrochemicals (that means they are by-products of gasoline production). You can find all-natural water-based lubes that might also contain herbs, flower essences, and additional skin-soothing ingredients like aloe vera or seaweed.

Silicone lubes are a bit messy (they can stain sheets and take soap and water to remove from the skin), but lots of people really like the fact that they are very slippery, and they work longer than water-based varieties. Silicone lubes are also safe to use with condoms and can be found in a variety of formulations. Look for chemical- and preservative-free varieties.

Oil-based lubes are absolutely not condom compatible, as the oil molecules will break down latex. Coconut oil and olive oil are common bases for these kinds of lubes, and flower essences and essential oils are often additional ingredients.

Oil-based lubes smell and taste better than either silicone- or water-based versions and are ideal for use during pregnancy.

Condemn the Condom?

The jury seems to be out on whether or not commonly available commercial latex condoms are biodegradable. The problem is that most waste (including condoms) that could break down in landfills doesn't, because a crucial ingredient to help decomposition—air—is eliminated when garbage is stacked on top of itself. While latex is a natural substance (it's produced by the rubber tree), it is mixed with stabilizers, preservatives, and vulcanizing (hardening) agents when made into rubbers, which renders them difficult to break down. Even under ideal circumstances, it would still take a latex condom many years to biodegrade. Polyurethane condoms are definitely not biodegradable, but lambskin ones are (but, animal-skin condoms don't prevent diseases, only pregnancy, and animal rights advocates might denounce them).

Whether they break down or not, using condoms is inherently eco-friendly; preventing pregnancy, and therefore not adding to the human population, is one of the most planet-positive actions you can take. Just make sure to dispose of condoms in the trash, NOT down the toilet. Most flushed condoms are fished out when wastewater is treated, but sometimes they're not, and they can make their way into waterways. Condoms have been found among sea grasses, draped over coral, and in the stomachs of fish and birds, which is unhealthy for them besides being extremely, extremely gross. Wrapping condoms in a tissue and tossing them in the trash means that they won't end up where they don't belong, and that they may eventually biodegrade. Make sure the wrapper goes in the trash too; even those made of foil are not recyclable.

natural Chompers

You might not eat your toothpaste, but you inevitably ingest some of the pasty stuff every time you brush. However, the long-term health effects of ingesting toothpaste have never been tested, since technically it's not supposed to be swallowed. If this doesn't bother you, perhaps the warning found on the back of most mainstream toothpastes instructing you to call poison control if you swallow more than "a pea-sized amount" will. Most commercial products are loaded with saccharine (which was found to cause cancer in lab animals), artificial colors and flavors (some of which are also potentially carcinogenic), and preservatives. And while the American Dental Association suggests fluoridated toothpaste is best for everyone, some natural health practitioners disagree, citing a higher incidence of bone cancer in people who regularly ingest fluoride.

Natural toothpastes, on the other hand, are made with natural sweeteners (like xylitol, which is made from birch trees) and do not contain chemicals. Instead they use baking soda, peelu (a vegetable fiber), and/or glycerine to get the gunk off. Depending on the brand, silica and bamboo powder are used for whitening, and an independent review of natural toothpastes shows that they are as effective as (and in some cases better than) mass-market brands. Essential oils are also added to some natural toothpastes for gum health and to help deal with sensitive teeth.

Some people have a little trouble making the switch from the über-sweet and hyperflavored commercial toothpastes to natural toothpaste. If you are going to make the switch, start with a toothpaste flavor and formulation (gel or paste) that is similar to what you're used to. Don't jump into the fennel or clove flavors right away; start with mint or cinnamon. Try mixing a bit of the old paste with some of the new for a few days, and then you'll be more used to it when you make the switch. Once you've gone through a tube of the natural toothpaste, try the old stuff again; you'll be unpleasantly surprised by the fake taste.

Don't forget that your toothbrush has an impact too; consider a recycled (and recyclable) toothbrush called Preserve by Recycline. These toothbrushes are made from the tops of Stonyfield Farm's yogurt containers. If you can't find recycled, pick a toothbrush with the least packaging and plastic, which also tend to be the least expensive brush on the rack.

Make-Your-Own Toothpaste

It might sound weird, but you'll save a bundle and won't sacrifice dental health if you make your own. I used this for about ten years when I was growing up and never had a cavity! It's easy:

1. Combine two to three drops of (preferably organic) peppermint oil to three tablespoons of baking soda and one tablespoon of table salt.

2. Add two teaspoons of glycerin (available at drugstores or craft stores, since you can also make soap with it).

3. Mix it all together and keep in a covered container so it doesn't dry out. You'll have fresh-scrubbed minty breath for just a few cents a week, and you won't be sending toothpaste tubes to the landfill. If you're not into peppermint, you can flavor your paste with other oils, like clove, cinnamon, or

spearmint. Or you can mix them; I love peppermint and cinnamon together.

Recycled Toilet Paper is NOT Made from Old Toilet Paper! (So Don't Worry, and Enough with the Jokes!)

You might already know that recycled TP (and facial tissue,
and paper towels) aren't made from old toilet paper, but did
you know that plenty of companies that make toilet tissue
harvest the wood pulp (from which paper is made) from trees
in old-growth forests? Ancient forests are home to trees that
can be hundreds of years old and support specialized ecosystems that are rapidly disappearing due to aggressive deforestation. It seems incredibly stupid to destroy an entire ecosystem
simply to wipe your butt. Unfortunately, it is usually the
super-soft squishy TP (and tissues) that are the worst offend-
ers in this department, so avoid those for sure. Don't worry,
I'm not suggesting you go without! Instead, look for toilet paper and tissues with recycled content.

There are many toilet tissues that are made from 100 percent recycled paper and they aren't hard to find. Even household name brands (especially Marcal) use recycled content, so
check the back of the package. While you're reading, keep in
mind that not all recycled paper is created equal. Two types of

recycled paper are found in paper products such as TP, napkins, and paper towels. Postconsumer content comes from the paper we all recycle in offices and homes, while preconsumer content comes from recycling paper scraps within the paper factory (which they would do anyway, since it also saves money), so opt for those tissues with the greatest percentage of postconsumer content possible. Same goes for facial tissue. If your local supermarket doesn't offer recycled products, ask the manager to start stocking them. You can always make a request for a certain type of product at the supermarket; that's how plenty of new things get to the shelves! Think about it; if you want recycled TP, there is bound to be other people who want it too!

The Chemical-Free Face: All-Natural Makeup

As you use up what's in your makeup bag over the next weeks and months, seriously consider replacing drugstore or department store brands with natural products. You only have one face, so why expose it to more chemicals than you already do? Toxins abound in the air and water throughout the world, and there's not much you can do to avoid them unless you stop breathing (or move into a bubble)! But you can minimize the chemicals you put on your skin, which is the body's biggest organ. It protects us from bacteria and viruses and helps rid the body of toxins.

Think about it: What happens to your lipstick as it wears off? Where does it go? Besides leaving a print on glass edges, or maybe on your honey's cheek, most of it gets eaten. Imagine chowing down on your lipstick—that's basically what you're doing whenever you put it on, just really, really slowly. Some estimates say that in the average lifetime, a woman will consume about four pounds of lipstick! Along with the inert ingredients like petroleum-based waxes and oils that make your favorite lipstick or gloss glide along your lips, you're also ingesting artificial colors and preservatives, some of which have been linked to cancer in lab animals.

Check out the two makeup options on the next page. With two different looks, you'll see you can go from girl-next-door to glam using makeup that's nontoxic, safe for sensitive skin, and isn't tested on animals. (You can still check out the hottest trends for makeup in the fashion mags, if that's your thing—I've found it pretty easy to replicate almost any look by using natural cosmetics.) Keep in mind that it's what you put on your face regularly that makes the difference, so if there's a really cool sparkly eyeshadow that you like to wear when you're out dancing once in a while that's not all natural—go for it! You can compromise, especially on the small stuff. But for everyday makeup, lotions, and sunscreens, go for products that are good for both you and the Earth so you'll look gorgeous while reducing your environmental impact. Always start with a clean, moisturized face before applying makeup!

Face 1. Mostly natural: Try Bare Escentuals 15 SPF mineral powder (made from naturally occurring minerals) on the face, Burt's Bees lip color in rhubarb (flattering on pretty much everyone), and a few swipes of Origins Full Story mascara.

Face 2. Knock-'em-out glam: Alchemy of Color Mineral Cosmetics makes a foundation powder, perfect for when you need more coverage. Afterglow Cosmetics makes bronzers (in three shades for all skin tones) and blushes (in five shades). Aveda and Alima both make the best all-natural eyeshadows and eyeliners in a huge variety of colors and wears (pearlescent, matte, shiny). If you want a rich, deeply colored lipstick, Colorganics Hemp Organics lipsticks are made with 85 percent organic ingredients and come in thirty-two different shades and colors (with lots of funkier shades included). Dr. Hauschka makes an incredible thickening mascara called Intermezzo (in black, brown, and electric blue!) and liquid eyeliner for an all-out look.

eco chick essentials

If you like shopping for makeup online, you have plenty of choices. KaiaHouse *(http://kaiahouse.com/)* is my favorite place for finding a great selection of makeup and natural care products (for both men and women), though they tend to be higher-end brands and a little more expensive. Each product is individually screened for toxic harmful chemicals like parabens, sodium lauryl sulfates, and others and is checked to make sure it's animal and environmentally friendly. Sephora (*http://www.sephora.com*) now offers a selection of natural and organic facial care products as well as mineral makeup. Other natural products like those mentioned above are easily found on large shopping sites like Amazon and MSN Shopping by searching under the company name.

Making Scents?

Commercial perfumes have huge advertising budgets, movie star promotions, and super-cute bottles. But most of them also contain phthalates, which help the scents stay fresh longer. If you've noticed that you usually sneeze when using nonnatural perfumes (I always do!) it's probably the phthalates causing that reaction, which I think is your body's way of saying "Keep Out!" Phthalates have been linked to cancer and hormone disruptions in rats, and are implicated in reproductive disorders in both men and women.

Try natural flower and plant oils instead. They can be found at most health food stores, natural foods supermarkets like Whole Foods and Mrs. Greens, and even at the mall at The Body Shop or Origins. Not only do the scents last longer on your skin, but you can also mix and match them to create a totally unique aroma, so that nobody else smells just like you!

Safety Note: Be sure you buy oils that are safe for use on the skin. Some oils are meant for burning or vaporization but shouldn't be used as perfume. As long as it says "pure essential oils" (organic if you can find it), you should be getting the real deal. Whether or not you have any allergies or sensitivities, before you rub any oil all over yourself it never hurts to first do a skin test with a tiny amount of any oil you haven't used before.

TOP TEN MOST DELICIOUS ESSENTIAL OILS

1. Lavender—relaxing and calming
2. Rose—classic; mix with other oils if it seems too "grandmothery" to you
3. Ylang-ylang*—exotic floral
4. Vetiver—like damp Earth
5. Chamomile—calming; a mild, sweet scent great for mixing

6. Sandalwood—sweet, woody, and warm
7. Jasmine—tropical and flowery
8. Grapefruit*—refreshing and pungent
9. Lemongrass—herby and lemony
10. Bergamot*—spicy orange

*Can cause photosensitivity, so don't use if you will be spending long periods in the sun or using a tanning bed.

How To: First, experiment with the scents you have. On cotton swabs or tissues, add just one drop of each scent, then put it in a clean glass jar, and let it sit for a couple of hours. Smell what's inside the jar. Is one oil too strong? One too weak? Try adding more or reducing the proportions of each oil until you have a scent you love. Next, mix these essential oils with sesame oil or extra-virgin olive oil in the glass container you want to keep your perfume in. Try using about one-fourth to one-third of a cup of oil, and start with five drops of each essential scented oil, then increase those that you want to be stronger. Gently shake the bottle and apply. Use common sense and your nose to guide you further. You can also use this oil in the bathtub!

When Aunt Flo Comes to Visit

Having your period is not a dirty thing, but we all know that sometimes it can get messy, and I'm not the only one who likes to avoid that. But using a bunch of super-wasteful, polluting, and possibly unhealthy products to deal with it is not the answer.

The average woman will have 450 periods in her life, which adds up to a lot of tampons and pads. Not only is that quite a bit of waste, with sanitary napkins ending up in landfills and sewer systems (and hundreds of thousands of tampon applicators washing up in coastal areas), but making these products also requires serious processing. The only way to make tampons and pads super-white is to use chlorine bleach. This bleaching not only creates water pollution waste, but there is also some evidence that even the industry standard elemental chlorine bleaching could cause dioxin to be leached into the body at very low levels. The Environmental Protection Agency says there is no safe level for dioxin exposure. Dioxin is a carcinogen and frequent exposure to it—like regular tampon use—can cause problems, including hormone disruption and immunity issues. And then there are the other artificial materials in tampons, which were mostly discontinued after several women died and many were sickened in the 1980s from toxic shock syndrome. However, rayon is still used, and some public health advocates suggest it can still cause health issues (not to mention that it's not biodegradable). All the major brands (Kotex, O.B., Carefree, Stayfree, Tampax, and Always) use rayon in their tampons. Tampons also contain chemicals like aluminum, fragrances, and alcohols, which can be irritating or drying.

A simple way to avoid dioxins, chemicals, and reduce the waste from your pads and tampons is by using 100 percent organic cotton, chlorine-free versions, and applicator-free tampons. Several manufacturers of these, including Natracare, Pandora Pads, and Organic Essentials, are available online and at natural foods stores and even in some regular drugstores. Seventh Generation makes chlorine-free pads and tampons with recycled plastic packages, and natural (but not organic) components. You could also try reusable pads, made from organic cotton, like Lunapads and EMA pads. These can be thrown in the wash and are great for those light-flow days when you would normally use a panty liner and don't really need a whole pad or tampon.

If you're comfortable with your body, and looking to use a no-waste, totally reusable system, the DivaCup (silicone), The Keeper (natural rubber), and the Moon Cup (medical-grade silicone) are small devices that fit inside your body and catch your menstrual flow in a cup; you just rinse and replace them, and they last for up to ten years, making them very inexpensive to use over time, with no waste generated at all. Apparently they are very popular with young European women. Another option are reusable, sustainably harvested natural sponges that are shaped to fit a woman's body and work like tampons, sold under the company name Jade and Pearl, proving that having your period doesn't have to be a wasteful, polluting proposition.

? Not So Stupid Question #1

I want to use natural bath products, but I'm afraid of breaking the bank. How can I go organic on the cheap?

One of the easiest ways to get great natural products without spending a lot is to buy in bulk. Though it will be more expensive initially, you will end up paying less over time, and you'll get the added bonus of using a lot less packaging. Kiss My Face, Nature's Gate, JASON, and Dr. Bronner's all make large jugs of body wash and moisturizer that will last for ages. You can always pour some into smaller containers for travel or if you don't want huge jugs cluttering up your shower. Get a sibling, roommate, or live-in partner to share with you, and you'll both save money and keep water resources (and your skin and hair) clean.

Two

All About Eco Fashion

M ost of us have figured out that organic food is healthier for our bodies and the planet, but clothes are another story: as a friend of mine once said when I suggested
she buy an organic cotton T-shirt, "Why organic clothes? I'm
not eating them." This chapter will explain why organic and
sustainable fabrics are worth the cost, and how you can also
look super-fantastic in them.

Why Eco Chicks Give a Damn About Fabrics (or Where Those Hot Jeans Come from and Who Makes Them)

Producing clothes has a big impact on the planet, directly affecting the health of the people and the local ecosystems where
the fibers that make up fabrics are grown or manufactured,

dyed, woven, styled, and shipped from. Each part of the creation of a pair of jeans, say, demands a different set of chemicals and produces waste. To cheaply produce a cotton T-shirt, one-third of a pound of pesticides and herbicides are used; polyester, rayon, and acrylic are made from petroleum; and wool, leather, and silk are taken from animals and insects, all of which use resources and produce waste. But don't freak out; that doesn't mean that to be an Eco Chick you need to go naked (or even worse—dress unfashionably)! There are plenty of greener options when it comes to fabrics, and lots of hot designers—from couture to mainstream—are working with them. But first, here's what you need to know to make you a smarter shopper and help you ask the right questions when you see an "eco" label hanging next to the size tag.

Looking at how the cotton plant gets turned into a pair of $150 must-have denims is a perfect lens for understanding what's not so great about many aspects of the clothing industry. Jeans are the staple basic in everyone's wardrobe these days, and for good reason: there's nothing easier than throwing on your favorite butt-enhancers with a cute top when you're late for a date, visiting your mom, or checking out your favorite new band. They basically go with everything and work for (almost) any occasion. But before those great new jeans get zipped up for the first time, they go through myriad processes and many people's hands to get to you. Let's follow a pair of jeans from start to finish and find out what's *really* between you and your Calvins.

There are three main processes that occur when producing a piece of clothing: source material (see more details on fabrics, page 37), production methods, and shipping. Jeans start off as cotton plants, waving in the breezes of countries like India, China, Pakistan, and Turkey, all places that have trouble enforcing environmental and pollution rules, even if they're on the books. Unregulated pesticides, herbicides, and fertilizers are used to grow the plants, water is taken from local rivers for irrigation, and fertile land that could be used to grow food for local populations is instead utilized to grow cash crops like cotton.

After the cotton is picked, it has to be dyed; cotton grows naturally in shades of green to brown, so synthetic indigo is added to make "blue" jeans. The darker the jeans, the more dye is used. Rivers and streams that were once clear are also turned blue when the jeans are washed after they are dyed and the toxic indigo is dumped into waterways. (Pictures of dark blue water being excreted from jeans factories are depressingly easy to find.) Next the dyed cotton is spun, woven, and may be treated with special finishes. In order to make the fibers easier to work with, a host of chemicals are used, and lots of energy is needed to run the machines that do much of the work at this stage. Finally, jeans are "styled," which includes all those details like stonewashing or extra stitching. Some jeans are stonewashed using chemicals, adding to the toxic soup that goes into a mainstream pair of denims—and also into the local water supply where they are manufactured.

The people who do all the processing, dyeing, and

stonewashing of those jeans often aren't treated any better than their local environments. Even companies that say they monitor the conditions of their factories can be very lax about enforcement, letting factories continue to operate that repeatedly fail to meet agreements about workers' conditions. The majority still don't pay even the minimum wage for the countries that they operate in. Clothing companies that make jeans say that they have to make them competitively priced, but less than 10 percent of the retail price has anything to do with the cost of making a pair, and only 2 percent of the price is attributable to labor. Especially when people are paying upward of $100 for denims, it seems worth a couple of extra bucks (one estimate of the cost to make sure that workers are paid a fair wage is about two dollars per pair) not to destroy a local ecosystem or take advantage of the people who live there.

Now you know why it's totally worth the extra effort to go planet-friendly with your high-waisted hot pants, skinny jeans, stovepipes, flares, bell-bottoms, and daisy dukes.

Green Shopping Basket

 There are lots of great organic denims, and new companies are jumping in every day. You can start by looking at Loomstate, Levi's Eco line, Del Forte, Of the Earth, and Kuyichi.

What's Up with My Shirt Being Made of Corn? Can I Eat It?

There are many fabrics and combinations of fabrics available that claim to be Earth-friendly or otherwise "natural." There is no official labeling system for fabrics, as organic food has, though there are some independent governing bodies that use a variety of labels. Here's a breakdown of the fabrics you're most likely to see advertised as "sustainable," "eco-friendly," or "environmentally sound."

ORGANIC COTTON. This cotton is grown without the use of chemicals, pesticides, or artificial fertilizers. Traditional cotton needs gallons of chemicals per acre to grow successfully; organic cotton farmers use complimentary forms of pest control and rely on less environmentally damaging means of growing and picking the cotton.

COLOR-GROWN COTTON. Undyed. The colors you see are the natural shades that cotton grows in, which vary from cream, to green, to a light brown. This cotton is usually organic and has a very low environmental impact because it bypasses the chemicals inherent in growing and dyeing traditional cotton.

SILK. Production, for the most part, is environmentally friendly. Silk is made from the cases of silkworms. (But for the insect lovers out there be aware that to get the fibers, live silk moths are thrown in boiling water; for a single silk shirt thousands of worms are killed.) Recently, several companies have begun producing silk that does not entail killing the cocooned silk-worm, by letting the moths emerge from their cocoons, and then using their cases to make fabric. Look for labels that either say "peace silk" or "vegan silk" if you are looking for this kind of fabric.

WOOL. Can be an eco-friendly fabric, but usually it isn't, unless the sheep are organic. Sheep need to be dipped regularly in insecticides, and breeding over thousands of years by human beings has led sheep to develop a host of diseases, for which they are regularly treated with antibiotics and other medicines—which can make their way, via sheep poop, into local water supplies and wild animals' systems. Once sheep are sheared, a very stressful and sometimes bloody procedure, their wool then has to be stripped of the lanolin that is inherent in wool. To get this protective fat out of the sheep wool, it must be treated with very strong detergents, which also can end up in local water supplies. Finally, the wool must be bleached or dyed, using additional toxic chemicals.

ALPACA. Different from wool, which is taken from sheep. Unlike sheep, which have been bred for thousands of years for both their meat and their coats, alpacas need little human intervention in their natural life cycles. They don't need regular doses of insecticides for their fleece, and they need less medical intervention due to their hardier systems. Alpacas leave a light footprint on Earth (literally, they have padded feet that don't destroy pasturelands), and they don't need as much food, which means less or even no fertilizer for their food crops. Alpacas are shorn like sheep for their coats, so if you don't like the idea of human beings using animals for their fur, then you won't like alpaca any more than sheep's wool.

INGEO. A new human-made fabric from fermented plant sugars (usually corn), which, depending on whether it's grown organically or not, could have a negative impact on the land and water surrounding the crop. However, Ingeo uses up to 50 percent less energy than cotton to create the fabric, reducing global warming gases significantly as compared to traditional fiber weaving.

BAMBOO. Grows quickly and easily, needing few or no chemicals to keep a crop healthy. (Not all bamboo is eco-friendly; sometimes native forests are removed to plant it, so look for sustainable bamboo.) When made into fabric, it is naturally antibacterial, which means that it won't hold on to body odor (making it an especially great material for socks and underwear). Bamboo is also very soft, almost like cashmere, but not as fuzzy, and drapes beautifully.

POLYESTER. Traditionally made from petroleum (a nonrenewable resource), but some newer versions of the fabric are made from recycled plastic bottles or recycled polyester fabrics. Fleece outerwear is made from polyester, so look for those that are made from recycled fibers rather than from new, petroleum-based ones. Vintage polyester from the 1970s is still with us, as it keeps its color and shape quite well; another eco-friendly choice is reusing the fun polyester prints that are still out there by incorporating them into a modern wardrobe, or using the older fabric in new designs as a detail or trim, which is a favorite of many eco-fashion designers. Look for vintage polyester in thrift stores, consignment shops, or vintage clothing boutiques.

TENCEL. A brand name for lyocell, which is a fabric made from wood pulp. It's biodegradable and recyclable since it's made from cellulose (plant fiber). Its production process involves lower emissions and less wastewater than other manufactured fabrics like rayon or polyester and needs no bleaching, unlike cotton. Tencel is naturally wrinkle-free and soft, and lets the skin breathe.

SOY FABRICS. Made from the protein by-products of soy oil manufacture. The longer-than-usual fibers of the soy plant make for very soft clothes; soy is often used for bras, undies, socks, and pajamas.

HEMP. There are a lot of misconceptions floating around out there about the hemp plant. Let's clear away the smoke from the pretty flowey hemp pants.

WHAT HEMP IS: a fast-growing fibrous plant that needs no pesticides, herbicides, or chemical fertilizers. Industrial hemp is super-tough when woven into fabric and can be funky and rough or smooth and drapey like linen, but less wrinkly (especially if it's mixed with another fabric, like organic cotton). Hemp seeds and protein can be found in foods, and hemp is the plant that was historically grown in the United States to make all sorts of useful stuff (rope, cloth, even our first dollar bills!). While currently it can't legally be grown in the United States, plenty of other countries, like Canada, recognize the eco-friendly value of the hardy and useful hemp plant, and *it is totally legal to buy products made from hemp in the United States.*

WHAT HEMP ISN'T: Hemp is NOT marijuana, Mary Jane, dope, weed, ganja, herb, or pot. You can't smoke it. (Well, I guess you could, but nothing would happen.) The hemp plant that's used to make clothing, and whose seeds are used in baked goods, cereals, and even to make a soylike drink (hemp milk, anyone?) contains only minute amounts of THC, which is the chemical in the cannabis plant that makes you feel goofy when you smoke it. Eating (or wearing) hemp has as much to do with getting high as eating a poppy seed bagel has to do with smoking opium.

PROFILE OF AN ECO CHICK
Fashion Designer Carol Young

Carol Young's high-end fashion line, Undesigned, is inspired by art and nature and filled with eco-friendly elements—but you'd never know it from looking at her stuff. Every season she comes out with a line that is wholly unlike the one that came before, with a modern classic aesthetic. Carol explains her line below.

What's in a Name?: Undesigned is created for the urban nomad—clothing that travels well, works in a variety of urban environments, is flexible in style (day to evening), and has properties that allow one to move and commute using personal mobility or mass transit.

I like my designs to be part of a "system" that works together in one's wardrobe, season to season. Environmentally, I think it's important to design/buy/wear pieces for your wardrobe that will last, be made of materials that don't require too much dry cleaning, and are durable, comfortable, and practical. At the same time, they should be beautiful and individual.

Fave Fabrics: I use eco-fabrics including knit and woven organic cotton, soy, bamboo, recycled cotton and fleece, Tencel, and hemp. My favorites are the organic cotton fleece (super soft and cuddly), bamboo and soy jersey blends (very comfortable and drapey), and recycled soda bottle fleece (cuddly and warm).

Designer surplus fabrics add the spice to the collection. These fabrics are leftovers from other manufacturers and are available in limited quantities. I purchase them to round out the collection and add color/pop. These have included silk-flocked dots, optic dot polyester charmeuse, novelty tweeds and denims, fine silks, and wool suiting. Sometimes these are used in little hidden areas, such as pockets, trim, and facings, to add an extra special touch.

Inspiration: I love having the opportunity to collaborate with other artists and filmmakers because they feed the soul. All of my collaborators are also good friends, and I brought up the idea of doing films with them as a purely fun/creative outlet for all of us.

How to Be Like Carol: Focus on learning design and process first. Choose fabrics wisely, and get as much life experience as possible (I've worked all sorts of retail jobs and internships, as well as been an English teacher in China and worked at an architecture firm). Travel to third-world/developing countries—this is such a humbling, eye-opening experience that will change your worldview. Also, make sure you're having fun!

ECO QUICKIE.

Thomas Edison's first lightbulb used a filament that was made of carbonized bamboo. It's still burning today; you can visit it at the Smithsonian Institution, in Washington, D.C.

Labels, Labels, Labels!

Labels do tend to become confusing, so don't feel bad if your brow gets awrinklin' when you're not sure what they mean. To keep it simple, there are three kinds of labels:

1. Labels whose rules are made—and checked—by a verified government source. For instance, in the United States, organic food must meet certain rules that the Department of Agriculture has decreed.

2. Labels whose rules are made—and checked—by independent verifying organizations. These organizations are usually nonprofits that are independent from the companies that use their designations and stand as watchdogs over the industry. Fair trade labels fall into this category.

3. Self-labeled or unverified labels. Some companies will slap an "all natural" label on products, and while they may not be lying exactly, these labels tend to mislead. For instance, cotton isn't synthetic, so technically it's a "natural" fiber. But as we've seen in the previous section, there's plenty that's unnatural and downright polluting about cotton grown nonorganically. Other labels are sometimes used for clothes and food, and you should ask about them. Sometimes a given product can't "officially" be labeled by an independent or government orga-

nization because they haven't gone through all the steps necessary to be considered; or the process might be prohibitively expensive for smaller companies (this is true with the Organic label); or it might take a long time to become certified (newer companies face this limitation); or a company might fulfill some, but not all, of the requirements to receive a certain label. Keep this in mind when you are trying to determine what labels mean when you're shopping. Below are some of the major designations.

FAIR TRADE: There is no U.S. certification for Fair Trade goods (though there is an official one for coffee and chocolate; see chapter 9). Internationally, this label is governed by two main organizations. IFAT (the International Fair Trade Association) insists that its member companies comply with ten standards (which include accountancy transparency, gender equity, fair pay, and environmental responsibility) over their product lines. The Fair-Trade Certified Cotton label references cotton products only, and the label is issued on a product-by-product basis.

ORGANIC: You might be familiar with the USDA's Organic label, but their oversight only extends to food and, to a lesser extent, personal care products. Clothes can use the logo if the crops used to make them were certified organically grown (you'll see this with cotton especially, since it is also a food crop used to make cottonseed oil). But that says nothing about what happened to the fiber after it was grown and could mean that toxic dyes or finishes were used. But these are still better than unlabeled garments. There are quite a few organizations that oversee organic fiber production, especially in Europe. Look for: The Soil Association's logo, Skal's EKO label (Dutch), and marks from IMO (Swiss) and AGRECO (German). These organizations are all part of IFOAM, which is the International Federation of Organic Agricultural Movements.

LOCALLY SOURCED: This is a label you might come across that's not overseen by any group. Usually it indicates that materials and manufacture of the item come from the local environment, reducing CO_2 emissions and assisting communities.

ALTERNATIVE FIBERS: Could mean anything from hemp, bamboo, and silk, which are only somewhat alternative, to really interesting stuff like flax, nettle, corn, or soy. Either way, supporting fabrics other than polyester and conventional cotton is a good way to encourage the fashion world to diversify, and most alternative fibers are less environmentally destructive than conventional ones.

RECYCLED: Not an official label, it usually indicates that some or all of the garment is made from materials already in existence. This could mean anything from creative reuse (utilizing vintage fabrics or factory extras) to full-on conversion of one thing into another (like grinding up old sneakers whole and making them into new sneaker soles).

SWEATSHOP FREE: Not an official label; in the United States it sometimes means that the clothing was made with union labor. For items made in other countries, it probably means that there is some consideration for workers' rights, but you will have to rely on the information the company presents when deciding whether or not to buy.

ETHICALLY PRODUCED: This label is uncertified by any entity and may mean something similar to Fair Trade or Sweatshop Free.

> **eco chick essential**
>
> Vintage clothing can be a fun way to add some color, variety, and interest to your wardrobe. I've been a Goodwill and Salvation Army devotee for years—the more rural and random the location, the better the stuff. Once you find a gorgeous piece from the 1940s, 1950s, 1960s, or 1970s that fits well, you'll likely keep it for years. On eBay you can also find some amazing vintage sellers, who give detailed measurements, pictures of clothes on models, and close-up image details, so you will have a pretty good idea of what you're getting. To find vintage on eBay, don't go to "Women's Clothing," but from the main page look under "Clothing, Shoes and Accessories," then go to "Vintage" and then choose from "Women's Vintage Clothing" or "Women's Vintage Shoes" or "Vintage Accessories."

Lingerie for a New Millennium

Your lingerie is the clothing that is closest to your body—don't you think that it should be as clean and pure as it can be? If you've read through the previous section on labels, you know all about eco-fabrics and why they're so much better for the environment. These fabrics, like organic cotton, soy, organic silk, bamboo, recycled polyester, and even fiber made from trimmed white pine branches are all used to make bras, panties, robes, and nighties, from simple white versions to lacy and racy ones. Next time you find yourself looking at the holes in your underwear and know you need to invest in some new ones, check out one of the online stores below.

UNDERGARMENT UPGRADE

Enamore (*http://www.enamore.co.uk*) offers cute knickers with lots of lace and flirty details, all made from organic silk.

Butta (*http://www.butta-inc.com*) has some simply sexy tanks and undies made from antimicrobial (and therefore stink-resistant) bamboo. Sewn and produced by an African fair-trade cooperative.

Patagonia (*http://www.patagonia.com*) makes recycled polyester microfiber undies and sports bras that are ideal for the hiking, mountain-biking chick.

Gaiam (*http://www.gaiam.com*) has several organic cotton underwear choices (with just a bit of Lycra for stretch) and pretty nighties and robes.

Figleaves, the giant knickers retailer, now has a green section on its site called Greenleaves (www .figleaves.com) with cute camisoles, bras, pajamas, tights, and robes.

Chickie Tip: Dreadful Dry Cleaning?

Conventional dry cleaning involves a range of toxic chemicals, but the nastiest is perchloroethylene, known casually as perc, and 95 percent of dry cleaners use the stuff. Not only is it bad for you, but it's even worse for the people who have to clean your clothes and who are exposed to it all day, every day. Perc is a chemical that causes liver and kidney damage, and is a known carcinogen. Make sure to air clothes cleaned this way outside for a few minutes before bringing them into your house, where perc can hang out and lower the quality of indoor air.

Look for clothes without the "dry clean only" label so you don't get into the expensive cycle of having to take clothes to the cleaners. If you have to dry clean, look for a "green cleaner" in your neighborhood—they're popping up all over these days. A green cleaner will either use wet cleaning (supposedly 99 percent of "dry clean only" garments can be washed this way), silicone and CO_2 solvents (not that common), or hydrocarbon solvents like EcoSolv or D-2000. Both of these are petroleum derivatives, so wet cleaning is the most Earth-friendly choice.

You can avoid dry cleaning by using Dryel, Custom Cleaner, or FreshCare products, which allow you to deodorize and do minor stain removal and then "clean" the clothes in your dryer at home. Though these products aren't particularly environmentally friendly, they are preferable to a dry cleaner who uses perc. Often you can just air out clothing, by leaving it hanging outside in a breezy spot or hanging it in the bathroom while you shower. Certain items labeled "dry clean only" can be hand washed, but it's a bit of a gamble; I usually wash cashmere, wool, and mostly cotton blends (95 percent or more cotton) by hand and lay them flat to dry, but most other synthetic fabrics will get misshapen or shrink if exposed to water, so take care washing them yourself.

ECO QUICKIE.

Perc persists in the environment long after your "dry clean only" sweater is dirty again. Surveys of U.S. food samples have found perc in grape jelly, chocolate sauce, wheat, corn, and even breast milk since about 90 percent of it persists in the atmosphere when it is used.

Super Fabulous Eco-Fashion

The great thing about planet-friendly threads is that these days there are so many different types available, so if you want to wear organic clothing you won't be relegated to yoga pants and T-shirts. Check out Anja Hynynen suit jackets and dresses for formal work environments or Linda Loudermilk for couture evening dresses. Loyale made a splash with the first organic faux-fur jacket, and speaking of wet and wild, Kelly B. makes some seriously hip swimsuits. For beautiful, funky heels, check out Charmoné, and for comfy, casual, but still interesting togs, check out Under the Canopy. Toggery specializes in solid jersey dresses and tunics that go with everything, and Doie makes flirty, easy-to-wear bamboo frocks. You can find all of these designers' wares, and up-and-coming eco-fashions, at brick-and-mortar stores and online boutiques. These are my top favorites, which tend to be like mini eco-clothing malls online, selling accessories, clothes, and shoes. A few have men's stuff too!

Online:

Kaight (*http://www.kaightnyc.com/*)
Greenloop (*http://www.greenloop.com*)
Beklina (*http://www.beklina.com*)
BTC Elements (*http://www.btcelements.com/*)
Adili (*http://www.adili.com*)
Modify (*http://www.shopmodify.com*)
Sodafine (*http://www.sodafine.com*)
Coco's Shoppe (*http://www.cocosshoppe.com*)

Offline:

New York City
Kaight, *http://www.kaightnyc.com/*
Sodafine, *http://www.sodafine.com*
Ekovaruhuset, *http://www.arcadiaboutique.com/*
Gomi NYC, *http://www.gominyc.com*

Boston
4March, *http://www.4march.com*

San Francisco
Eco Citizen, *http://www.ecocitizenonline.com*

Washington, D.C.
Setchi, *http://www.shopsetchi.com*

Chicago
Pivot, *http://www.pivotboutique.com*

Philadelphia
Arcadia Boutique, *http://www.arcadiaboutique.com/*

Vancouver
Dream Designs, *http://www.dreamdesigns.ca*

Three

Reduce, Reuse, Accessorize!

The right accessories can turn the same jeans and T-shirt ensemble from nice and preppy to Rock-and-Roll. Just like clothes—and for many of the same reasons—shoes, bags, belts, jewelry, and scarves can have a huge or negligible environmental impact. Good thing there are so many designers and do-it-yourselfers out there coming up with super-creative ways to funk out your regular wardrobe. From bags made from candy wrappers or old billboard posters to sandals constructed of juice drink containers and belts made of vintage coins, accessories are all about creative reuse. Of course, vintage bags and shoes are always in style, and if you look in the right places, you can even find some that have never been worn before.

Before and After Accessory Makeover

You can look just as great with eco-friendly alternatives to what you might normally buy, no matter what the season. This doesn't mean you should get rid of all your old accessories and buy new ones. Use whatever you have to mix and match with newer bags, belts, and shoes that are easier on the planet's resources. Think eco-friendly fabrics, vintage finds, and even a fun DIY project.

Summer

Before

Basic jeans and white tank

- PVC flip-flops (manufacture of PVC releases toxins into the air and water)
- Large plastic beach bag (plastics take hundreds of years—or more—to biodegrade)
- Gold earrings, bangles (mining practices for gold are notoriously polluting; see page 65 for more info.)
- Plastic hair clip
- Disposable water bottle

After

Same basic jeans and white tank

⊙ Recycled PET flip-flops (made out of PET, no. 1 plastic soda bottles!)

⊙ Renewable raffia handbag (look for materials that are natural renewable resources, like straw, raffia, jute, or hemp; bonus—they will biodegrade too)

⊙ Huge over-the-shoulder beach bag made from old ship's sails (filled with organic cotton beach towels of course)

⊙ Vintage gold earrings and bracelet (no new precious metals need be mined; see more info on page 65)

⊙ DIY cloth hair scarf (make your own from a favorite old T-shirt, curtain, or pillow, and you'll have a totally unique accessory)

⊙ Stainless-steel reusable water bottle (comes in fun designs and keeps plastic bottles out of the waste stream—only about 30 percent of which are ever recycled, so carry your own instead)

Winter

Before

Basic jeans and black cowl-neck sweater

⊙ Wool scarf and hat (wool processing requires polluting detergents and dyes)

⊙ Knee-high boots (leather tanning is super-toxic to the workers who make the boots)

- ◉ Large leather bag (ditto for leather bags)
- ◉ Chunky silver ring and bracelet cuff (silver mining has a negative impact on ecosystems, just as gold does. See page 65 for more info.)
- ◉ Hot Java in disposable cup from coffee shop

After

Same basic jeans and black cowl-neck sweater

- ◉ Cute pumps made from naturally tanned leather, or a mix of non-PVC synthetics, recycled materials, and vintage textiles. Some are even built so that they are endlessly repairable, so you don't end up chucking them after a season!
- ◉ Fleece scarf and hat made from recycled soda bottles
- ◉ Clutch made from recycled candy wrappers
- ◉ Big bag made of recycled leather handles stitched out of leather from old cowhide couches and unused textiles from the 1950s.
- ◉ Bracelet made from recycled silver and natural river stones
- ◉ Stainless-steel thermos (with Fair Trade, Organic coffee inside!)

Great Bagspiration

A great bag will make an outfit and can be the most fun, visible way to make your ensemble more interesting and stylish. Bags make a statement, carry your stuff, and can add a pop of excitement to an otherwise ho-hum ensemble. There are amazing eco-friendly bags available, from vegetable-tanned leather messenger bags that you'll still be carrying when you retire (what could be more planet-friendly than an accessory that lasts twenty or thirty years?), to fun, bright designs made from natural plant materials, to organic cotton totes, to really creative stuff-haulers made of recycled gum wrappers, juice boxes, old sailboat sails, discarded billboard posters, chucked bike tires, and even excess car seat-belt material. Searching online is an easy way to find unique, handmade, and recycled wallets, iPod cases, handbags, backpacks, and more. You can even find bags with solar panels built in that will charge your phone or laptop with the sun's energy.

There's also nothing easier than making your own bag at home. Bags are just sacks of whatever size suits your fancy, and even if you don't know how to sew well, and don't own a sewing machine, you can make your own carryall. Look around your home, place of work, friend's houses, and thrift stores for unusual materials. Be creative and look for:

Old pillows or curtains with interesting patterns
Stained clothes (you can use the unstained portion of
   the fabric)

Used kids toys (stuffed animal fur can become a funky trim)

Paint-splattered tarps

Denim in various colors and washes

Vintage cloth napkins

Ladies' handkerchiefs from the 1930s, 1940s, 1950s, and 1960s

Once you've found a few fabrics that you think are fun, try mixing and matching them, and you can find patterns online to create your own bag. Once you see how easy it is, you can make them for friends and relatives, or even sell them online!

Green Shopping Basket

 Looking for a great bag? Try: Reusable Bags (*http://www.reusablebags.com*), World of Good (*http://www.worldofgood.com*), Bazura Bags (*http://www.bazurabags.com*), Ashley Watson (*http://www.ashleywatson.net*), Entermodal (*http://www.entermodal.com*), Mad Imports (*http://www.madimports.org*), Ecoist (*http://www.ecoist.com*), and Envirosax (*http://www.envirosax.com*).

Eco Shoes: Leather vs. Pleather—What's Better for People, the Planet, and Animals?

There's not a woman I know who isn't a little obsessed with shoes. They can make you appear taller and slimmer, support you on long walks, keep you dancing all night, and maybe create a rhythm for your day as you click-clack along. They also seem to go in and out of style faster than anything else; platforms are de rigueur one season, flats are the "it" shoe the next. Or it's square-toe pumps one year and round-toe the next, and then back to square again, maybe with a quick detour through pointy-toe territory (though they are tough on the feet and never seem to stick around long). Because of these shifting styles, our culture tends to view shoes as disposable, and many shoes are made that way, which isn't good for our feet or Earth's resources.

So what to look for in an eco-friendly shoe? First off, aim for a pair that will last. Whether it's flip-flops or knee-high boots, shoes should endure for more than a season, so look for styles that aren't super-trendy and are made well. This doesn't mean you have to don Birkenstocks all summer and recycled rubber nurses' shoes all winter. There are plenty of shoes that will meet your style requirements and fashion sense without stamping on the environment or depleting essential resources.

So first a word or two on what's used to make your fashion

footwear. When it comes to shoes, many people automatically think leather. Leather is technically a by-product of growing animals for meat. Whether or not you believe in using animal products in your daily life is up to you (see more details in chapter 7), but if you are going to buy leather, there are a few things you should know.

1. Just because a label says "leather" doesn't mean it came from a cow. If the shoes were made outside the United States, the labels "cowhide" or "genuine leather" are not vigorously regulated. Shoes could be made from pig's skin, goat, horse, sheep, dogs, cats, or any other animal unlucky enough to be around when leather was needed.

2. There are responsible leather producers, whose leather comes from reputable vendors and whose shoes are usually called "vegetable tanned." You'll see this label on eco-friendly leather products, and it means that instead of harsh and polluting leather tanning (tannery chemicals are known carcinogens and water polluters), the leather is treated with vegetable-based products that have a lighter impact on the Earth. This process is more time-consuming, so this kind of leather will be more expensive, but not outrageously so. Eco-friendly leather shoes may also be dyed with natural plant-based dyes or have decorations that are made from sustainable materi-

als, like recycled wood or natural fibers, or vintage fabrics.

If you decide that leather is not for you, or you simply want to try something different, there are lots of great alternatives out there. Nonleather shoes can be made from a variety of materials, including "pleather" (human-made plastic that looks like leather), a tough fabric like hemp or organic cotton canvas, or even recycled rubber or used car tires. A few eco-pointers:

1. Pleather shoes are often (but not always) made from PVC, which is short for polyvinyl chloride. PVC is not such great stuff; when it is made, while it is being used, and once it is disposed of, PVC gives off dioxins, which every human being on Earth (not to mention animals) now carry in their bodies. It has even been found in the breast milk of Inuit women in the Arctic Circle. Dioxin is a compound produced by chlorine-containing industrial processes (like the manufacture of PVC) and is a known carcinogen and a hormone disruptor; some scientists believe it is responsible for reproductive problems in humans. I try to stay away from PVC and plastic in all areas of my life.

2. PU (polyurethane) plastic is also sometimes marketed as pleather; it is also environmentally damaging, and both PU and PVC are petroleum based,

which means that one of their ingredients is crude oil, a nonrenewable and rapidly dwindling resource.

3. Your best nonleather eco-friendly bets are shoes made from materials other than plastic, though recycled plastics, like EVA, can give you the look with a lower impact. Wood and cork (hopefully harvested in a responsible manner; look for a label that says so or visit the company's Web site) make great platform heels, and for summer shoes, especially, there are plenty made from materials like jute, bamboo, and cotton. When thinking winter boots, investing in a high-quality pair in leather or pleather that you

---

Green Shopping Basket

Eco-Friendly Shoe Companies

Simple Shoes Green Toe line (*http://www.simpleshoes.com/greenLanding.aspx?g=greentoe*), Cydwoq (*http://www.cydwoq.com/*), Charmoné (*http://www.charmoneshoes.com*), Terra Plana (*http://www.terraplana.com*), Mink Shoes (*http://www.minkshoes.com*), Mohop Shoes (*http://www.mohop.com*), Tom's Shoes (*http://www.tomsshoes.com*)

Online Shoe Stores

Moo Shoes (*http://www.mooshoes.com*), Via Vegan (*http://www.viavegan.com*), Vegan Store (*http://www.veganstore.com*)

---

keep in good condition and wear for many years might be a compromise that will keep your feet happier than trying to make a go with shoes that don't properly protect your feet from the cold. You'll just toss them after a few painful wearings, which is no good for your wallet or the landfill.

A SHOE MAKEOVER

I've seen my friends throw out plenty of perfectly great shoes because they were scuffed or had a worn heel or sole. Unless shoes are totally unwearable, there are a few things you can try before you toss them in the trash.

1. It's a good idea to polish your shoes to keep them supple and water resistant, but if you've got shoes that are looking trashed, polish can save them as well. Invest in a good shoe polish and give them another chance. I am not kidding when I say that you will be absolutely shocked at how good shoes can look again after being polished—like new or close to it.
2. A broken or worn heel or sole is definitely not reason to add your shoes to the landfill; getting them

repaired will save money and resources. Plus, you won't have to break in a new pair of shoes!

3. Sometimes you fall out of love with shoes you've just bought, or they just never fit well; if you have a lightly worn pair collecting dust in your closet, donate them to Goodwill, Salvation Army, or a local thrift store. For used sneakers, check out Nike's Reuse-a-Shoe program, which recycles sneaks of any brand and makes them into playground surfaces.

eco chick essential

Superpages is a really useful Web resource for finding local shoe repair. Just go to *http://www.superpages.com*, type in "shoe repair" and your zip code, and a whole list will come up, along with a handy map showing their locations.

Green Shopping Basket

Organic Coconut Oil Shoe Polish from Po-Zu (*http://www.po-zu.com/eat.html*), Nike's Reuse-a-Shoe Program (*http://www.letmeplay.com/reuseashoe*)

Bedecked and Bedazzling: Jewelry That's Naturally Beautiful

Suffice to say that if your favorite accessory is jewelry, your fetish might not be so pretty once you know its history. Simply put, those gold earrings, that platinum and diamond ring, or silver choker all come from raw materials that have to be mined from the Earth, and the extraction of metals and gems is not only hard on the environment, but it's also not much better for the people that do the dirty work of digging these precious metals and gems out of the ground.

Many countries where metals, gems, and semiprecious stones are mined are poor and have few laws to protect the environment and do little to enforce them due to the costliness of policing a profitable industry. Diamond, gold, silver, and platinum mining opens gaping holes in the Earth that are usually not remediated once the mine is used up, and mining also pollutes the water, as topsoil and mine "tailings" (toxic chemicals) wash into surrounding waterways. I've seen a gold mine firsthand in the United States, where there *are* regulations, and let's just say "destroyed landscape" pretty much sums it up. In countries where there are few or no rules, not only are environmental concerns flouted, but safety rules are usually ignored as well.

The majority of diamonds are the result of the backbreaking labor of the African people who mine them (who make about thirty dollars a week officially, but usually make half that) and the Indian people who cut and polish them (the average price to cut a stone is about twenty-five cents). You may have heard the term "blood diamond" to refer to the stones that come from mines in impoverished countries, and the term is not hyperbole. Diamonds have been and continue to be used as currency to fund wars: rebel leaders in Sierra Leone have used diamonds to pay for weapons that have thus far killed 75,000 and left twelve million homeless. Because Americans buy 65 percent of the world's diamonds, you can bet our lust for the gems has financed murders.

The good news is that there are tons of gorgeous jewelry already out there to accessorize with; vintage jewelry can be fabulous and less expensive than the new stuff, and some artisans even make new designs using parts from old jewelry. There are literally piles of existing jewels and metals out there, and even ethically mined and Fair Trade stones and metals have to be dug out of the Earth. No matter how supposedly environmentally sound the operation, mining is a dirty, ecosystem-destroying process. I avoid all new jewelry unless it is made from recycled materials or nonmined components.

If you must have a new diamond, there is the option of buying them, as well as precious metals, that meet Fair Trade and ethical and environmental mining standards, though some industry watchdogs say that the rules here are hard to track and enforce. The Kimberly Process was a voluntary agreement signed by diamond-producing countries in 2003 that is supposed to result in a document for every diamond sold, showing that the diamond was ethically mined, but it does not take into account environmental issues. The Canadian government has strict rules about mining diamonds, concerning both workers' rights and environmental effects, so many jewelers sell diamonds from Canada and call them "conflict-free diamonds" or "ethical diamonds." There are no such industry-wide international agreements for mining of precious metals, though specific companies do make certain assurances and guarantees.

There are also quite a few jewelers that melt down exist-

Green Shopping Basket

Kristen Muenster *(http://www.kirstenmuenster.com/)* Designer Muenster only uses recycled metals and personally sourced semiprecious stones to create her clean-lined, earthy, modern jewelry.

Moonrise Jewlery *(http://www.moonrisejewelry.com/)* is like an ethically produced bauble mall, with necklaces, rings, bracelets, and even a wedding section.

Verde Rocks! *(http://www.gwen-davis.com/verde/)* Gwen Davis uses antique and recycled elements to create up-to-date jewelry with a vintage twist.

Leber Jewelers *(http://www.leberjeweler.com/index.php3)* offers Canadian diamonds and other gems sourced by the Leber family and employees, who work with suppliers to determine exactly where their rubies, emeralds, and sapphires come from.

ing gold, silver, or platinum to make entirely new, modern pieces, without having to participate in environmental destruction for their art. So go for vintage, reworked, or recycled jewelry and you won't have to wonder how much pollution or slave labor went into making your baubles.

Chickie Tip: Repair It!

We all like to buy new stuff (even if it's vintage) to add to our wardrobes, but the most Earth-friendly thing you can ever do is keep using an existing bag, pair of shoes, necklace, or belt, rather than buying new. I like to buy high-quality clothes, and especially accessories, and hold on to them. Not only do they gain a patina of age over time (something you just can't pay for), but they also become part of how people see you and your style. Whenever I lose an earring hook, or a bracelet catch comes disconnected, I take it to my local jewelry store for repair. (Chain stores aren't usually interested in doing this kind of work, so look for a family-owned establishment.) I repair my bags when the handles start to wear, or replace just one tired part of a bag or belt instead of the whole thing. Historically, it was much more common to fix things than throw them away and buy new ones, which is just really wasteful; it's one old-fashioned idea we should definitely make cool again.

part two

your nest

Your home is your sanctuary, no matter if you live solo in your own apartment, share one with roommates, crash with your parents, or buy a house on your own or with a partner or friend. Your living situation is uniquely yours, but however you live, there are tons of ways to be fabulous and have a great time in your space while still reducing your impact on the environment. If you're serious about fighting climate change, air and water pollution, reducing pesticide and herbicide use, being healthier, and protecting wildlife and open space, there's no place like home to start.

This is the largest section in this book because living in a sustainable way at home can have the biggest positive impact on the environment. From how to throw a less-wasteful party, to help in choosing the right houseplant, to figuring out what cleaning products to use, to what impact your birth control might have on your health and the environment, this chapter tackles the nitty-gritty of everyday living so you can make smart decisions about your home. And you'll have the info to back up those choices, so when people ask, you can fill them in.

You don't have to do everything that's listed here, nor will every option apply to you or your living situation, but take the opportunity to be inspired! You probably already have some idea of what you are doing that may be wasteful, such as using more energy than you need or producing more garbage than you know you should. Start with what you know, and as you read through you'll pick up additional information and tips you can apply to your home life over time.

Four

Home Eco Home

Your home is one of the only places in your life that you have a significant degree of control over. And even when you move, most of your stuff comes with you, so what you choose to buy for your abode will be around for a while. These purchases matter to both you and the Earth, which is impacted not only by the consumables you purchase—like food, bedding, furniture, and appliances—but also how you use them. If you combine conservation, recycling and reuse, smart shopping, and a little elbow grease, you can have a healthy, happy home to enjoy now and into the future.

Kitchen

If you're like me, you spend a lot of time in your kitchen—cooking, eating, cleaning, and staring into the fridge in wistful denial at 2 A.M.!But seriously, the most bizarre thing about the kitchen is that it seems to be the place where we eat, AND also use the most chemicals, most of which we *choose* to use! Cut your chemical habit, save money, and clear the air by choosing natural cleansers, or make your own. You can also reduce the chemical load on your body by eliminating disposable products and keeping plastic bags and containers away from your organic veggies.

Pots, Pans, and the Canary in the Coal Mine

What you cook your food in has an impact on how it tastes, as any chef will tell you. But what many folks are just now realizing is that cookware can also leave additional chemicals behind in your food.

Any cookware with a nonstick finish (especially if that finish has been nicked, scratched, or otherwise perforated) should be discarded. The main problems with nonstick surfaces, commercially called Teflon, is that it off-gases when heated to high temperatures, which has led to the deaths of hundreds of pet birds and an unknown number of human illnesses. The Environmental Working Group ran their own tests on Teflon-coated pans, which were followed by independent testing by a university food-safety professor. They found that "at 680°F Teflon pans release at least six toxic gases, including two carcinogens, two global pollutants, and MFA, a chemical lethal to humans at low doses." Four of the chemicals released from heated Teflon never break down in the environment, and most of us are carrying them around in our bodies. If it's killing birds, I don't want it in my kitchen. Do you?

Stainless-steel pots and pans are better than nonstick, but since they're made from a combination of metals (steel is an amalgam of nickel, chromium, and other metals) they too can leach into your food, though probably at negligible levels.

Some choose to avoid aluminum cookware because of aluminum's connection in animal tests to Alzheimer's. Anodized aluminum is preferable, as it keeps the metal from getting into foods and creates a nonstick surface, and this type of cookware is a personal fave of celebrity chefs.

Cast-iron cookware is not only safe, but it also has health benefits; it actually adds iron to our diets, a necessary element for production of red blood cells. This is the cookware I use the most in my own home. Though people say cast iron requires more upkeep than other types of pots and pans, I haven't found that to be the case, though you can't put iron pans in a dishwasher. Cast iron is not expensive, and you can often find it used and season it yourself! Seasoning cast iron is not rocket science; you simply rub the whole pan with olive oil and bake it at medium heat for forty-five minutes every once in a while.

Ceramic is another safe choice, though it tends to be a little more costly. It doesn't add anything to foods cooked in it, and because it is enameled to the metal underneath, it can come in a variety of colors. This cookware, like iron, lasts forever and can be put in the dishwasher.

Copper is another very safe option, and it's super-efficient because it heats up quickly. Though it needs to be cleaned well after every use, it looks really pretty hanging from a rack. Chefs love copper because it heats very evenly.

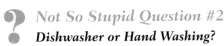

Not So Stupid Question #2
Dishwasher or Hand Washing?

The surprising answer is that if you have a newer, efficient dishwasher that doesn't require a lot of prerinsing, and you run it only when it's full, dishwashers actually use less water and power than hand washing. Not to mention that a dishwasher is a huge time-saver.

Just Say No to Bags!

These days it's definitely trendy to bring your own bag to the grocery store. Not only are canvas and mesh bags cute and stylish, but you can also pack a lot more into them (meaning fewer trips from the car to the house). They are also sturdier and more protective of your yummies than plastic or paper.

If you ride a bike or walk to the store—and kudos if you do! We should all aim to eliminate the car from routine activities like grocery getting—a large, roomy backpack is ideal for trekking your things home so you don't get shoulder strain from carrying too many bags in your hand, and you won't have to use one of those rolling granny carts (unless you want to).

Even if you bring your own bags to the grocery store, you may find other types of bags stacking up around the house: shopping bags from clothing stores, produce bags, small paper bags from the liquor store or drugstore, and plastic bags from the hardware store or take-out place. Some of these you can eliminate by carrying a slightly larger bag or tote for your main bag. I carry a bigger bag most of the time, in which I can fit purchases from the drugstore, a bottle of wine, a couple of books, or other small- and medium-size purchases. I politely decline the bag that store clerks want to give me, and I've never had a problem with this tactic. If you're not into carrying a big bag (I love them even when they're half empty), there are several companies that make bags that are totally collapsible or take up little space that you can fit into a side pocket of a smaller purse. That way you have an extra bag when you need one, but when you don't it folds down to the size of a large pack of tissues.

Paper or Plastic?

What if you've forgotten your reusable totes at home and have to choose between paper or plastic in the store? Neither choice is great; paper bags are made from trees, and they weigh more and take up more space, meaning that it takes more fuel to get them from the manufacturing plant to the grocery store. Plastic bag production means toxic chemicals are spewed into the environment, and they create such ubiquitous litter that some cities have now outlawed them.

The maybe-not-so-obvious answer is: if you have to, choose the bag that you'll reuse the most. I use plastic grocery bags for garbage can liners, so if I forget my canvas bags at home, I know I'll give the plastic ones another life as garbage bags. Do you need to recycle your magazines and newspapers in a paper bag? Do you use paper bags to make textbook covers, or for wrapping paper? If so, they might be the best choice in your household. And depending on the bags that you like to carry the most, you could just bring those back to the store again and again until they wear out, which is another alternative to bringing canvas sacks.

De-Plasticize Your Kitchen

It seems like there's plastic everywhere these days—from artificial limbs and fake boobs to credit cards and funky bangles. While not all plastic is bad, much of it is not so good, because any production of plastic releases all sorts of toxins into the environment (what kind of toxins depends on the plastic). Plastic is also made from petroleum, a nonrenewable resource that often requires intense, destructive processes to extract.

The place where you really want to cut down on plastic is in your kitchen, especially limiting its use for food storage. That's because when manufacturing the plastic various chemicals called plasticizers are added to the mix that becomes the bag, storage container, or disposable silverware. Plastic wraps and containers can leach these plasticizers, some of which are phthalates, a class of chemicals found in polyvinyl chloride (PVC) products. The World Health Organization considers these chemicals probable human carcinogens.

Especially when heated in a microwave, these chemicals can leak into food (especially fatty foods like meats and cheeses). While plastic food containers that say "microwave safe" are monitored by the FDA (only small amounts of toxins are allowed by the government to leach into food, amounts they say are negligible), if you are reusing plastic containers, such as take-out containers and plastic tubs (think of the kind buttery spreads come in) or yogurt cups, STOP! These plastics were not made to be used in the microwave or hold heated food and will leak nasties into your leftover lasagna or Chinese delivery dim sum. Also avoid heating plastic wrap. (It's kinda okay to use if you don't let it touch your food, but never zap something wrapped in plastic!)

So what *can* you use? I've switched over to all-glass storage and heating containers, which handily go in the oven OR microwave (sans their plastic covers if they have them, of course). To keep food moist when I nuke it, I cover it with a cloth napkin, or parchment paper, or paper towels if I'm away from home and don't have access to my regular supplies. Being a busy person, I love the convenience of using the same container for baking my tofu and veggies in the oven and then putting it in the fridge, but now I just use glass instead. It's a small switch that will eliminate yet another venue for chemicals to get into your body.

Uh-Oh! Someone's in the Kitchen with Vermin . . . and It's You!

Don't be embarrassed, it happens to everyone, no matter how clean you are, especially if you live in anything like an urban area. You have food and warmth, and mice, rats, ants, or roaches want some too. They haven't survived this long because they're stupid creatures, but before you reach for the poisons and the insecticide, try a less toxic approach.

MICE AND RATS. Whatever method you choose, DON'T buy the traps with the sticky goo that adheres to rodent feet, trapping them in place until they starve to death. No matter how much you don't like rats and mice in your home, there is no excuse for animal cruelty. A more humane method for keeping small mammals out of your space are sonic devices that use high-frequency sound waves to annoy pests away. You will need a few units, and responsible companies will admit there are limits to this technology, which include how much territory one device can cover. Make sure you follow directions and think about eliminating or reducing anything a sound wave can bounce off of, like pillows and blankets—these devices work best when their sound waves can bounce off hard surfaces. Havahart traps are another choice: they trap the mice and you can then take them to a park or the woods and let them go.

ROACHES. Even an animal- and insect-lover like myself has a problem with the roach, so I understand the impetus to freak out and run for the nastiest-looking bottle of roach killer your supermarket carries. To get rid of them sans toxic chemicals give your place a very thorough vacuuming—roaches love piles of dust and crumbs. Then make sure as many cracks as you can track down are sealed up, so you can block where they're coming in. Roaches hate catnip, so sprinkle this in the areas where you see them. You can use boric acid (which is natural but toxic to kids and pets, so use discretion about whether you want it in your home), and place barrier trails of it underneath the sink cupboard and on top of the kitchen cabinets. Also, spraying roaches (if they don't scuttle fast enough) with regular old soapy water will kill them. There are also nontoxic roach traps available.

ANTS. In the summer or when it's dry, these guys inevitably find their way inside. Most of the time they're looking for food or water, so make sure your counters don't have crumbs and that you don't have a leaky faucet. Frankly, if I see a couple ants, and they don't seem to multiply, I let it go—I have more important things to deal with, and ants are quite clean. But if you have a full-on ant parade marching across your countertop, you need to take action. Ants tend to stick to their trails, so if you disrupt their pathways, you can often get rid of them altogether. Identify their route and sprinkle peppermint oil, cayenne pepper, or white vinegar and water on it, removing any ants before you do so (I put them outside). If they tend to congregate in your sink or around the dog's water dish, try sprinkling cinnamon around the area—ants hate the spice, and your kitchen will smell lovely too.

SPIDERS. Arachnids inspire such fear in people, you'd think their job was terrorizing us instead of eating all the insects that really do cause us problems, like houseflies, mosquitoes, and moths. I actually have a "live and let live" attitude with spiders in my home, so they will eat pest insects, but if you can't deal, insert a clean vacuum-cleaner bag into your vacuum, suck them up, and take the bag outside and leave it for a day or so and let the little guys climb out to find a new home outdoors.

Green Shopping Basket

PestChaser (*http://www.sonictechnology.com/*), Havahart (*http://www.havahart.com/*), Active Roach Killer Bait (*http://www.roach-killer.com/roach-killer.html*), PestNOmoreroach Trap (*http://www.cmdproducts.com/pestNOmore%20B302.html*)

Want to remove insects from inside your house or apartment without harming them? All you need is a glass and a magazine. Place the glass over the insect and gently slide the magazine under them (be careful not to break their legs) and carry outside to release. You'll never have to touch a bug—or call a guy!

eco chick essentials:
Volatile Organic Compounds

VOCs are everywhere, both in real life and in this book, and while that doesn't make them trendy it does mean you need to know what they are and why they're baddies.

Volatile organic compounds are a class of carbon-based chemical compounds that have a molecular structure that enables pieces of them to come apart from the original molecule and float off into the air, which is called off-gassing. VOCs are found in new carpets, paints and paint thinners, dry-cleaning solvents, varnishes, plastics, adhesives, and furniture. They are generated by office machines like copiers and tobacco smoke.

Examples of VOCs include benzene, toluene, and xylene, which are all suspected carcinogens. VOCs can also cause immediate symptoms, including irritation of the eyes, nose, or throat; exacerbation of asthma; dizziness and nausea; and dry or itchy skin. In addition to being harmful to human and animal health, VOCs contribute to ground-level ozone pollution and global warming.

Living Areas

Your living room is where you entertain your friends, relax, snuggle with your honey, watch movies, and talk on the phone while IMing on your laptop, and doing your nails. In short, it's where you likely do your living and socializing when you're home. Most of us can't afford to redo a whole living room, but there are some eco-friendly choices you can make in this part of your abode, so when it comes time to upgrade a piece, choose a new rug, or repaint, keep these tips in mind.

The Big Stuff

Most of the large furniture we buy—coffee tables, couches, chairs, and entertainment centers—is the opposite of eco-friendly. They are often made from wood harvested from old-growth forests, glued together with enough chemicals to off-gas into your home for years, and covered in fabrics or painted with varnishes that add to the toxin load in your indoor air. You do have some options though; there are a growing number of "green" furniture manufacturers, and even popular stores like Design Within Reach are getting in on the planet-loving. Look for natural upholstery, FSC-certified wood (FSC is the Forest Stewardship Council and they make sure wood comes from sustainable forests), and all-natural varnishes or paints.

Another option is to reupholster your own furniture or fix up funky old antiques. I've recovered a whole set of my own kitchen chairs, as well as a set for a friend; you get to pick the exact fabric you like, and it's easy if the chair bottoms are removable. When I recovered an antique chair I inherited from my grandmother, I found some vintage fabric I loved and brought it to a professional upholsterer to do the work. Besides saving a piece of furniture from the landfill, recovering means you can find great eco-friendly fabrics with which to cover your chair, couch, or ottoman, and you can find the exact print you like and not get stuck with a designer's choice.

Pretty-Up Those Walls

You know that new-paint smell? What makes paint smell so strongly is the VOCs—toxic chemicals that are floating off into the air as the paint dries and for some time after. Look for low- or no-VOC paints, which are now available at pretty much all hardware and paint stores, large and small. There might be a slightly higher price margin for the non-toxic paint, or it may be the same price as the toxic stuff—prices have come way down in the last couple of years for these paints. Either way it's not much to pay to keep chemicals out of your home. And yes, you can still get any color you want (though very dark paints have slightly higher VOC levels), and unless you buy a no-VOC paint, make sure you still leave windows open to air out your newly painted space.

In addition to low-VOC paints (which look and act the

same as smelly paints), I've used Anna Sova's milk paint in my home, which smells like cake batter and is so nontoxic you can eat it! It looks a bit different from traditional paint—more matte and mellow—and has a distinctive soft finish.

You can avoid the mess, expense, and hassle of painting and repainting (especially if you live in an apartment where this will cost you) by using vintage fabrics and other material as wall coverings. Secondhand Indian saris and tapestries can add visual appeal and are very easy do deal with when you move. Vintage sheets and curtains can make great wall hangings—just make sure edges are finished neatly.

Rugs, Carpets, and Floors

The fewer rugs the better. If your wood floors are already under a wall-to-wall carpet, expose them and use areas rugs instead. Refinishing floors is a worthwhile investment if you're going to be in a space for a while. Look in your area for companies that use low-VOC varnishes. Or do it yourself by painting the wood with chemical-free paint (see section above), a very stylish way to have rug-free floors with panache.

Carpet holds allergens, dust, dust mites, and whatever you track onto them from outside, so using them only as accent rugs will cut down on your exposure. In addition, new carpets and rugs (unless they are all-natural) also off-gas VOCs. Wall-to-wall carpets are also pretty wasteful, because once the high-traffic areas of the rug are worn down, the whole thing needs to be replaced, and both the rug's good and used parts all end up at the same place: the landfill.

If you must cover a room wall to wall, consider FLOR, which is recycled and recyclable modular tiles of carpet (they

---

Green Shopping Basket

Furniture and Accessories: Vivavi (*http://www. vivavi.com*), Healthy Home (*http://www.healthyhome .com*), Design Within Reach (search under "eco-friendly" in the sidebar) (*http://www.dwr.com/*) Maku Furnishings (*http://makufurniture.com/*), Viva Terra (*http:// www.vivaterra.com*), Greenhaus (*http://www.thegreenhaus .co.uk*), Branch Home (*http://www.branchhome.com*)

Paint: AFM Safecoat (*http://www.afmsafecoat.com*), Ecos (*http://www.ecospaints.com*), Benjamin Moore Eco Spec (*http:// www.benjaminmoore.com*), Anna Sova Milk Paint and Wallfinishes (*http://www.annasova.com/sections/wallfinish/default .asp*), Old-Fashioned Milk Paint (*http://www.milkpaint.com/*)

Rugs and Carpet: FLOR (*http://www.flor.com*), Nature's Carpet (*http://www.nontoxic.com/purewoolcarpets/ naturescarpet.html*), Natural Home Products (Biohaus Carpeting) (*http://www.naturalhomeproducts.com*)

---

even have an all-natural fiber collection). As tiles become worn or stained, individual tiles can be replaced and the old pieces sent back to the company for recycling. FLOR tiles stick to each other, not the floor, eliminating VOC-producing adhesives, and they can be cut easily by hand to any size to accommodate fixtures and furniture. They come in a huge variety of colors, styles, and thicknesses too, which makes picking them out really fun.

chickie tip

Chickie Tip: Remove Your Shoes!

Take your shoes off at the front door or entryway to keep dirt and dust—as well as toxic chemicals used on streets and sidewalks—out of your home.

eco chick essential

Why buy new when you can barter, buy used, or borrow? When I needed a guest bed, I didn't buy a new one, I went on Craig's list, a national Web site *(www.craigslist.com)*, and found one that was inexpensive and barely used. Online services minimize sketchiness by hooking you up with people responsibly looking to get rid of their extra stuff. I met the guy I bought the bed from and could see from the circumstances that it was in good condition. When I move again, I'll probably sell the bed via the same site!

The Neighborrow site (*http://neighborrow.com*) is another great way to find or get rid of furniture (and sporting goods, yard tools, and even CDs and DVDs) by connecting with people in your community and trading stuff you need for stuff someone else needs. (The site figures all this out for you!)

Bedroom

Organic in the Bedroom: Sexy AND Healthy

Most people end up spending about one-third of their lives in bed, and there are few other places that we spend that much consistent time, so if there's one place to cut down on your toxin load, it's there. Looking at a mattress, you might not think there can be a big difference between an organic mattress and a regular one, but there is; it's just hidden inside. Building from the inside out, conventional mattresses are likely constructed from a chemically doused and unsustainably harvested wood frame, and like most furniture, held together with a plethora of chemicals, including formaldehyde and toxic glues and adhesives (which release VOCs; see page 83 for more info on these toxins). Then they're topped with conventional cotton and/or polyester covers, and the whole thing is doused with flame-retardants. All of these chemical baddies are released into the air and your lungs while you slumber on top of them, and lots of heavy-duty chemicals are needed to grow and process the cotton covers and fillings. Once you see your bed as a product of the industrial chemical industry it might make you a little bit restless.

Going organic when it does come time to replace your mattress (most are designed to last about ten years) is a simple way to remove toxins from both your home environment and the planet's. And these days, organic mattresses are not that much more expensive than the traditional versions; when I went online I found organic mattresses that were only about $200 more than conventional models. Spreading that cost over ten years, that means you only pay $20 per year for chemical-free sleep.

When it comes to bed linens, it's easy to go organic, from sheets, shams, blankets, and comforters that are printed with patterns and florals, to bright colors, varied textures, and even monogrammed sets. You can definitely find these online for the same price as conventionally grown cotton sheets, and there are sales on these items, so keep a lookout and you will score organic sheets for a great deal. And you'll rest easily on sheets that you know have been produced without chemicals to grow or dye them. (For more information on the specific benefits of organic cotton vs. traditional, see page 35.)

PROFILE OF AN ECO CHICK
Green Designer Jill Fehrenbacher:
Creating the Ultimate Eco-Friendly Bedroom
Jill Fehrenbacher is the founder and editor in chief of Inhabitat.com, an online magazine devoted to innovative sustainable architecture, products, furniture, interiors, home decor, and fashion. "I got my start in this because I'm a designer (graphic designer, furniture designer, and architect), and at the time that I launched Inhabitat, there were really very few resources

to help someone find out about sustainable design. So I decided to start my own publication devoted to the subject matter," says Jill. Inhabitat has expanded a lot since its inception and now covers home decor, products, and fashion in addition to architecture and interior design.

What are the top five eco-friendly changes to make in the bedroom without breaking the bank?

1. *Light.* Lighting is a fundamental concern in any room of your house, but it is super-important in the bedroom, where access to natural light can have a big effect on your sleep-and-wake cycles.

    Relying on natural light to light your room instead of electric lights can significantly reduce how much carbon dioxide you produce, can reduce your energy bill—and is also healthier for your body.

    To maximize daylight while also maintaining some privacy, look for blinds or curtains that are translucent and diffuse light, while still letting a lot of light in. Never use heavy opaque curtains or blinds that block the light. Japanese paper blinds are a great, inexpensive way to let light into your room while still maintaining privacy.

2. *Air quality.* This is a hugely important and mostly overlooked concern for the bedroom. If you have windows that you can open, do so for cross ventilation and try not to rely on air conditioners unless its absolutely necessary. They significantly dry out the air, as well as using a ton of electricity.

Avoid painting your bedroom and using hazardous VOC chemicals in your bedrooms (no turpentine, nail-polish remover, shoe polish, etc), and if you must, use low- or no-VOC paints and air your room out for twelve hours before you sleep in it. If you have any allergies, wash your sheets and duvet frequently, and consider using an air filter.

Candles produce a lovely quality of light and set a great mood in your bedroom, but they do a real number on the air quality and oxygen in your room. The best candles are made from natural materials such as beeswax and soy, with cotton wicks, and these are much cleaner burning than paraffin candles, because paraffin is a petroleum derivative. Cheap, poor-quality candles often have lead in the wicks, which can give you lead poisoning, and the soot given off from the smoke toxifies the air and can make it difficult to sleep. AVOID AT ALL COSTS: container candles (the ones in jars), candles made from paraffin (most cheap candles), and candles with lead wicks. If you must burn candles, use beeswax—and don't burn them very often or for very long.

3. *Bed comfort*. Good beds are worth the money, so be prepared to invest in one. Purchase mattresses made out of materials such as natural latex, wool, and cotton. Brands to check out include CozyPure, Natura, and Natural Organic. I'm currently obsessed with a Greek brand of mattress called Coco-matt— which makes the most comfortable mattress I've ever slept on. (I discovered it in a hotel in Rotterdam.) I'm currently trying to figure out how to get them to ship to the United States.

4. *Organization*. A cluttered bedroom can wreak psychological havoc on its occupant, so try to keep your belongings organized and out of sight. If you live in a tiny space with no closets (like me), create hidden storage space wherever you can. Clever space-saving solutions include bed frames with drawers built into them, tables, desks, and chairs with storage inside, and/or simply packing the space underneath your bed with Container Store–style drawers and storage solutions.

5. *Minimalism*. Keep bedroom decor to a minimum, and make sure you keep extraneous stuff from work or school out of your sleeping area.

How can one create a bedroom that is super-restful? I have more than a few friends who have problems with insomnia; how can they deal with this issue naturally?

Make sure your bedroom is set up only for sleeping; remove any electronics, desks, and distracting work-related objects. Keep computers, TVs, and other electronics out of your bedroom. They not only give off magnetic fields that can disturb your sleep, but you also want to psychologically create the space that your bedroom is for sleeping only, not for working, studying, eating, or anything else. Make sure your bedroom is quiet and dark at night.

In a dorm, decor can't be changed, so what else can one do to make that space personal and eco-friendly?

Sometimes when you are in a dorm room, there is not a lot you can do. The next best thing is to optimize and personalize the things that you CAN change, and make them the best they can be. This includes bedding, lighting, electronics, and decor. Make sure you have your own natural, high-quality comforter and bedding, as this can quickly put you at ease in an otherwise alien and generic space. Buy a nice LED desk or floor lamp. Christmas lights are an inexpensive dorm staple, and its now pretty easy to find cute LED Christmas lights that give off a calming blue hue. Finally, decorate your walls with pictures, posters, and even tapestries that reflect your personality.

Green Shopping Basket

You can find high-quality mattresses at: The Clean Bedroom (*http://www.thecleanbedroom.com/*), Savvy Rest (*http://www.savvyrest.com/*), and EcoBedroom (*http://www.ecobedroom.com/shop/beds.html.*). **Organic sheets can be found at:** Amenity (*http://www.amenityhome.com/*), Branch Home (*http://www.branchhome.com/*), Vivavi (*www.vivavi.com*). **For LED lamps:** Amazon (*http://www.amazon.com*), Target (*http://www.target.com*), Design Within Reach (*http://www.dwr.com*).

Five

Squeaky Clean and Toxin Free

We all want to be considered clean, but everyone's definition of that is a little different. For some of us, kitchen floors that shine and bathroom sinks always free of toothpaste and hair are necessary to feel comfortable at home. For others, as long as we can find our way to the bed at night and our clothes are clean we feel pretty on top of our life. Whether you are a clean freak or a bit of a slob, what you clean your place with matters. Cleaning products are some of the most toxic stuff we keep around, and while we know that it's healthy to keep bacteria and viruses out of our lives, it's also important not to overdo it with chemicals in your home environment.

Something to think about is: "What does clean smell like?" Your answer will probably depend a lot on what you grew up smelling when you knew something was clean. For many of us, clean smells like bleach, pine cleaner, and the chemicals in antimildew tile spray and window cleaner. Sometimes when people switch to natural products, which aren't packed with chemicals, they feel like their home is less clean because they have so long associated "clean" with the smell of these noxious chemicals. Ironically, introducing these chemicals into your home actually makes your home more toxic, since you are now breathing in a soup of lung irritants and subjecting your skin to their punishing effects when you pick up a sponge. How did we get to the point where polluting your indoor air with a plethora of chemicals—stuff that makes your eyes water and dries your hands out so they look like an old ladies'—how did we get to the point where this was considered the definition of "clean"?

I've lived in all sorts of situations, from solo to roommate to partnered and back again, and for the past ten years, I've used almost no conventional cleaning products. I've lived with men, women, and multiple cats and a dog. I keep my house pretty tiddy (certainly not spotless, but I enjoy cleaning), and I do all my scrubbing and mopping myself. I've almost never used unnatural products. My house doesn't look any different than if I had used conventional stuff, and nobody gets sick, so the cleaning I do is sufficient to keep pathogens at bay, which is the most practical reason to scrub up. So try out some natural cleaning techniques, and reassociate the smell of clean with orange oil, peppermint, and flower scents instead of toxic chemicals.

Makeover for the Under-the-Sink Toxic Crew

Do you know what's under your sink? If I had to guess, I would say that most people have a glass cleaner, a counter spray, dish washing soap, toilet cleaner, a kitchen sink scrub, a bathroom scrub, a mildew killer, drain de-clogger, and maybe bleach, ammonia, furniture polish, pot scrubbers, and more, depending on your household. Each formulation promises to save you time and make cleaning so much easier. But do they really? And if you add up how much they all cost, what's the damage? And if you think about all those chemicals, what's the damage to yourself and the environment?

The truth is that most commercial cleaning products contain a wealth of toxins, chemicals, and substances that are not only unhealthy for you and your family, but also aren't very good for Earth's waterways or soil either. Every time these products are used and washed down the drain, we're adding to the chemical burden of the planet. If a cleaner has a number from poison control on the container, chances are there is some pretty strong stuff in there. Do you really want that stuff in the same place you eat? Do you really want to breathe it in or let it get on your skin?

When air-quality experts test the air inside a home, they usually take readings of VOCs (volatile organic compounds) to judge how good or bad it is. VOCs can cause respiratory distress, exacerbate asthma, irritate nose and throat linings, cause headaches, and over time can be carcinogenic and stress your liver and kidneys to the max. Walking around randomly in most homes, VOCs register at about 50 ppb (parts per billion). Get under the sink though, and that number jumps—and that's with product containers closed and sitting quietly. Test the air after opening a container of bleach wipes, and the number can climb into the thousands (anything over 500 is considered problematic to asthmatics and others with sensitivities). VOC levels in disinfecting sprays can climb even higher; some have tested into the parts per million, instead of billion— which means seriously bad air.

While some products may not seem to bother you, and you figure you only use them a couple times a week anyway, keep your lifetime exposure in mind, because some of these chemicals accumulate in your body. Not only are you breathing them in every time you squirt (especially with sprays, as they float into the air as much as they land on the counter), but they are being absorbed into your skin when you touch them, and eventually, you are ingesting some of them from food and hands that touch countertops and sinks. If you walk around in bare feet in your home, whatever you clean your floor with and scrub your shower floor with ends up in your bed and on your couch. The cumulative exposures to toxins from different sources over many years is what some scientists believe is causing a rise in the incidents of cancer, hormonal problems, and reproductive issues.

So how do you know what the bad stuff is? Well, the cleaning product companies—and the government—don't make it easy for you. Like shampoos and conditioners, ingredient formulations are considered trade secrets, and apparently the companies' economic interests are more important to the government than consumers interested in protecting their health. So companies are not required to list ingredients. (In California, they must provide a warning if a product poses a significant risk of cancer or reproductive harm.) Many companies do include a partial ingredient list, or only include "active" ingredients, but it's really hard to avoid particular ingredients, since you can't really know if they are listed or not.

I say practice the precautionary principle; there may be no way to know (unless labeling laws change) if the exact combination of chemicals that are in a given product, or if exposures to those products, will cause cancer in your body. But because there are plenty of toxin-free alternatives, doesn't it make sense to take the precaution of eliminating as many as you can from your life?

KEEP OUT! (OF YOUR HOME)

Do your regular cleaning products have warnings on them (like those on the next page)? They probably do if they contain toxic chemicals, and most do. Use this guide to understand what the specific dangers are and consider: Do you really want these poisons in your house to make it "clean"? And if it's harmful in these quantities to a 180-pound man, what about you?

Caution: *An ounce to a pint* may be fatal or harmful if swallowed, inhaled, or absorbed through the skin by an adult 180-pound man.

Warning: *A teaspoon to an ounce* may be fatal or harmful if swallowed, inhaled, or absorbed through the skin by an adult 180-pound man.

Danger: *A taste to a teaspoon* is fatal if swallowed, inhaled, or absorbed through the skin by an adult 180-pound man.

ECO QUICKIE.

Asthma affects more than fifteen million people and is one of the most common chronic health problems in the United States.

What Do You Really Need to Be Clean?

You need only a few products to keep your house clean. Streamlining your myriad cleaning sprays, scrubs, and powders will save you money, time, and keep chemicals out of your home environment. Use up or give away what you have and start fresh by putting these ingredients on your shopping list:

- ⊙ Baking soda (get a big box!)
- ⊙ White vinegar
- ⊙ Citrus cleaner (try Citra-Solv or Orange Glo)
- ⊙ Soap (castile soaps in liquid form are my favorite)
- ⊙ Essential oil in your favorite scent (I like lemon, orange, or peppermint for housecleaning)
- ⊙ Use rags, sponges, and scrub brushes instead of paper towels and disposable cloths (like Swiffers) for cleaning, scrubbing, and polishing around the house and save the energy and the landfill space that's filled with these single-use items.

Throw rags in a cloth bag (not plastic, otherwise they will mold) when they're too dirty to use anymore and chuck them in the washer when you've got a load's worth. Sponges can be cleaned by running them through the dishwasher on the top rack every couple of days.

Cleaning Recipes

All-Purpose Cleaner for Floors, Toilets, and Walls

Mix one cup white vinegar, one-half cup baking soda to one gallon water. (You can store this concoction in a squirt bottle or large plastic jug.)

Spray Cleaner for Countertops

Dilute the great-smelling citrus solvent (easy to find in concentrated form at regular and health-food stores) in water per package directions and keep in spray bottle; make sure you shake the spray bottle a bit before each use to distribute the citrus oils.

Furniture Polish/Dusting Spray

Mix ten to fifteen drops of lemon, orange, sandalwood, or lavender oil (or whatever your favorite essential oil is) with a cup of water. You can keep it in a spray bottle or just dip a soft cloth into the mixture. This will get dust off your furniture, and the oils will scent and polish wood, plastic, or almost any household surface. (Only use special cloths on computer and TV screens, though you can clean electronic housing safely with this mixture.)

Window and Mirror Cleaner

Fill an old spray bottle (sixteen- to eighteen-ounce size) with three teaspoons of white vinegar, and fill the rest up with water. Use crumpled newspaper to wipe the windows or mirror down. (Newsprint prevents streaks, unlike paper towels.)

Scrub for Kitchen and Bathroom Sinks, Tubs, and Tile

I just use baking soda straight, sometimes throwing a little liquid castile soap on top, and scrub away with an old sponge (or scrub brush for the tub). Baking soda gets everything super-clean and deodorizes naturally.

Note: I don't make all my own cleaning supplies. Two items I don't make but am sure to buy in eco-friendly versions are dishwashing liquid (for the dishwasher, which you can't make yourself) or powder, and laundry detergent, both of which should be made without phosphates and artificial colors and fragrances. The reason we care about keeping phosphates out of the environment is that they don't break down easily and end up washing down rivers into the ocean, where they cause phosphate-dependent plants like algae and some seaweeds to grow out of control, blocking sunlight, which kills all the other organisms in the water. These algae blooms cause huge die-offs of fish and other aquatic creatures, and phosphates in cleaning products cause all of this destruction. The sad part is that phosphates are totally unnecessary for getting dirty things clean, so when you choose products without them, you won't be sacrificing cleanliness for healthy waterways.

eco chick essential

If you're not ready to jump on the make-your-own bandwagon just yet, there are some great companies that make delicious-smelling cleaning products. My very favorite is Mrs. Meyer's Clean Day (*http://www.mrsmeyers.com/*), which uses only natural essential oils for scent, including lemon verbena, and my personal weakness, geranium (how they get it to smell so good is beyond me). The Meyer's line can be found at health food stores, and Whole Foods. Method Home (*http://www.methodhome.com*) is another great green company whose products are available everywhere (like Office Depot, Target, Costco, and CVS) and has a low price point comparable to the traditional toxic brands and is perfect for things you go through quickly, like hand soap and all-purpose sprays. Heather's Natural & Organic Cleaning Products (*http://www.heathersnaturals.com/*) makes my favorite bathroom deodorizer spray, and their Oxygen Bleach Cleanser is the best I've found. (It works better than any scrub—conventional or natural.) All three of these companies don't animal test but do use ingredients that are biodegradable or break down into environmentally benign constituents, and are safe for children, pets, and pregnant women.

Dirty Problems/Clean and Green Solutions

Stuck Drain

Avoid, avoid, avoid chemical drain-cleaning products! They contain some of the nastiest solvents out there, including lye and acid. Try these four steps before calling a plumber to snake it out.

1. Plunge it! Make sure there is enough water in the tub, sink, or toilet to cover half the height of the plunger, and then let suction (and your arms) do the work. Give a few plunges and see if the water passes down the drain. If not, repeat once or twice, adding a bit of water if it doesn't work the first time, which will add pressure.

2. For tubs and sinks, simply removing the drain stopper and pulling out the gunk might solve the problem; the greatest percentage of clogs take place at the drain. It may be a little gross, so if dead hair and soapy goop bothers you, wear a pair of kitchen gloves. Use an unbent hanger to create a hook shape, and go fishing for gunk! It's actually kinda fun! You can prevent hair and food clogs in the first place by making sure there are filters or screens over all your drains.

3. If you don't have success clearing the drain by the above methods, try pouring one-third of a cup of baking soda down the drain, followed by one-third cup of vinegar. The chemical reaction (remember making volcanoes in elementary school science classes?) can break down soapy clogs. Follow with a kettle full of boiling water to cleanse the drainpipe. There are also eco-friendly bacteria-based drain cleaners out there; you can find them in health food stores and large natural foods supermarkets (and online, of course!).

4. For really stuck drains, when all the above methods fail, consider investing in a drain snake, which is a long, metal tube that "snakes" into drains and pushes the blockage through. You can find these at home improvement stores, and they are cheaper than calling the plumber.

Mildew

Mix one-quarter cup hydrogen peroxide with one-half cup water, and the juice of half a lemon. Mix and put in a spray bottle, then spray on the mold. Wait an hour to let the stuff work, then scrub off with a solution of baking soda and soap; spray off with water.

Baked-On Stove-Top Grease

Make a paste with baking soda, white vinegar, and a bit of water. Coat range and let sit for five minutes before scrubbing off.

Green Shopping Basket

Drain Cleaners: Earth Enzymes from Earth Friendly Products (http://www.ecos.com/), Dispoz-All Drain Cleaner (no Web site), Drainbo Drain Cleaner (http://www.drainbo.com/)

Orange Cleaners: Citra-Solv (http://www.citra-solv.com/), Seventh Generation (http://www.seventhgeneration.com), Biokleen (http://www.bi-o-kleen.com/)

Microwave Gunk

Combine a cup of water and two cups vinegar in a microwave-safe bowl and nuke it for two minutes on high. This will loosen dried and crusty food remains so you can wipe them off. (If there are still stubborn bits left, heat for another minute.)

Not So Stupid Question #3
Should I Be Using Antibacterial Soaps?

No. Unless you have been advised by a doctor or other medical professional to use an antibacterial product because of an immune system disorder or other health problem, you don't need to use these products. Antibacterial soaps, wipes, and gels (the most common is triclosan) are part of a widespread problem called antibiotic resistance. Because so many people are using antibiotics, the bacteria are actually mutating and becoming resistant to antibiotics. This is of serious concern because at-risk people who get bacterial infections are now left without effective medicine.

Quite a few researchers are now even hypothesizing— and they have some good evidence to back this up—that we are too clean. Our immune systems evolved to fight off bacteria and viruses, and when we disinfect every-

thing all the time, our bodies have nothing to do, so they attack themselves, which is why allergies are on the rise. Even the Centers for Disease Control say that good hand washing with regular soap and hot water is sufficient for preventing disease.

Six

Defeating Power Vampires

There are tons of smart choices you can make that will help you use energy more efficiently around your abode. If keeping global-warming gases and pollutants out of the air isn't impetus enough for making some, or all, of the changes in this chapter that you can, then plain old cash savings should motivate you. The average American can reduce utility bills by 65 percent by becoming very efficient around their house or apartment. And it doesn't matter whether you rent or own your house or apartment; the cash savings will be significant regardless.

If you don't pay for your utilities, don't let that be an excuse to waste them. Over 90,000 people a year die from respiratory diseases related to poor air quality that are the result of conditions created by electricity-generating power plants that use fossil fuels like oil or coal (and 85 percent of our power comes from these types of plants). Whenever I turn a light off, shut down my computer, or turn the heat down a couple of degrees, I think of how I'm clearing the air, just a bit, for everyone now, and in the future.

Saving Energy, Saving $$

Power vampires really suck. No, I'm not talking about those frenemies who have your back one minute when they need you and then desert you when you call on them. I mean something far more insidious (at least for our planet's air). Power vampires are all those little gadgets that we can't live without; our crackberries, cell phones, MP3 players, digital cameras, laptops (and any soon-to-be invented devices that will be necessities five years from now). These little electronic accessories that make our lives easier and more fun are also mini-energy suckers. Add a few together, and the time that they spend plugged into the wall after they're fully charged, wasting watts, is significant. Other power vampires include less-portable electronics that remain on or in standby mode all the time. All those little flashing lights and glowing buttons are just wasting power as they glimmer.

The good news is that there is a really easy, simple way to avoid all this energy sucking (dodging your fair-weather friends, not so much). Just buy (or ask around, people usually have extras of these they're not using) a few of those surge protectors or power strips. Plug all your rechargeable stuff into one, and after they're full up with juice, just flip off the one switch on the whole strip. Same goes with a computer setup or a home entertainment system. If the power strip doesn't have a switch, you can unplug the one plug from the wall, instead of unplugging each component individually. I have my TV, DVD player, antenna, receiver, and speakers all plugged into one strip. When I'm not watching a movie (about 99 percent of the time), the whole shebang is shut off with one flip of the switch.

Some newer devices are also being designed with an auto shutoff feature so that once they're fully charged, they power down automatically. Look for these features when you're upgrading your electronics. And make sure to unplug when you are at work, out of town, or asleep.

Appliances—It's Easy to Be Efficient

There are lots of great resources to tap into if you need to buy a new fridge, washer and dryer, dishwasher or stove. Remember that these purchases are going to last for years to come, so investing in one that you like and that will also save you energy will be well worth it. Do your homework before you go shopping; spend a bit of time online to see the price ranges so you won't be shocked, as well as to see what kinds of features are available (some will affect energy use; see breakdown below).

Consumer Reports' GreenerChoices site (*http://www. greenerchoices.org*) is a great place to start, as it gives details about how much energy and water an appliance uses in comparison to others. GreenerChoices also gives information about efficiency settings or available options that may be hard to find elsewhere. Remember that paying a little more when you buy a more efficient appliance could mean that it pays for itself in electricity savings in a year or even less, depending on how ancient the unit is that you're replacing.

The Environmental Protection Agency's Energy Star program (*http://www.energystar.gov*) is the standard that's used to compare various brands' efficiencies, and the site will also fill you in on what criteria were used to figure out the ratings. The easiest way to know that you are looking at an energy-efficient machine is to make sure it has one of those bright yellow Energy Star tags hanging from it. The label will show you how efficient a given machine is compared to other similar machines. The tags will also tell you how much, on average, the unit will cost to run for a year, which makes comparisons among choices easier. Think about how often a unit runs to get an idea of how much you'll save. Do you only run your dishwasher twice a week? Do you do a lot of laundry? Appliances that are on all the time (like refrigerators) are good candidates for replacement, and it's worth buying as efficient a model as you can afford.

Appliance Efficiency Breakdown

Washers and Dryers

- ⊙ Choose a front-loading washer over a top-loading version. They use half the water and a lot less energy, since gravity does much of the work; many say they do a better job at getting clothes clean, and there's less wear and tear on your togs too.

- ⊙ Gas-powered clothes dryers are much more efficient than electric, saving you serious cash, because dryers really suck up power. Gas dryers cost about $50 more up front than electric, but you will likely see at least this much in savings after just a year of using the more efficient machine.

- ⊙ Consider investing in a water extractor (or "spinner"). These dandy devices spin most of the extra water out of laundry before you put them in the dryer, cutting drying time in half (or more). You'll use so much less electricity (you do have to plug in a spinner) drying your clothes that extractors typically pay for themselves in three to four years. A bonus is that it's much easier on your clothes if the water is sucked out of them this way rather than tumbling them in a dryer, so your favorite jeans will last longer.

Stoves

- If you don't cook much at home, you might want to spend your money on upgrading other appliances rather than the stove and oven. If you are an amateur chef, the right choice of stove will save you time and money.
- Convection ovens are about 20 percent more efficient (and cook faster) than traditional ovens.
- Self-cleaning ovens are easier to clean AND are usually better insulated, making them somewhat more efficient than those without this feature.
- Ceramic glass on top of radiant burners is the most energy-efficient stove top.

Dishwashers

- Look for settings that will allow you to use less water. They are usually listed as "energy saver" or "power saver"; some dishwashers have specific settings for heavier loads (like pots and pans) and lighter loads, so take advantage of these options.
- Keep the heated dry setting turned off unless you need the dishes right away. Air drying is free, and even though my dishwasher manual says to use the heated dry, I've never noticed any difference by letting my dishes air dry.
- If you never seem to have enough dishes to fill up your dishwasher, think about getting a smaller unit

when you need to upgrade. Then you can wash more often without wasting water.

Refrigerators and Freezers

⊙ The fridge is the biggest individual energy user in most homes. This is one of the only times when replacing rather than repairing an old unit, even if it's still running, is a good idea. Definitely don't repair a vintage unit; it's just not worth it. Old fridges are so much less efficient than new versions it's ridiculous. (Energy Star's site says new refrigerators are up to 50 percent more efficient than those that are just ten years older.)

⊙ Don't buy a side-by-side fridge/freezer combo, as they are the least-efficient setup. The best is fridge on top, freezer on the bottom (since heat rises).

⊙ A half-empty fridge is less efficient than a full one; keeping food in the house will encourage you to eat more healthfully (and will probably result in fewer take-out containers to throw out!).

⊙ Many fridges are set too cold. Get a cheapie thermometer (or borrow one) and use it to adjust your settings to 35 to 40 degrees Fahrenheit for the fridge, and 0 to 5 degrees for the freezer. If your fridge has an "energy saver" setting, use that as a guide, but even these settings can be colder than necessary, so it's worth checking it out yourself.

- Make sure your refrigerator seals properly; even a tiny space can create significant cold-air drain, especially on warm days. Limit time spent with the door open by thinking about what you want before you open the fridge door.

Laundry Matters

Laundry seems to be an inherently wasteful process for many people, with lots of room for improvement. Follow the tips below to save time, energy, and money while still getting your whites white and maintaining a colorful wardrobe.

- Always wash a full load or use settings for small- or medium-size washes.
- Washing in cold water makes sense for most of us whose clothes just don't get that dirty. Not using heated water saves money and energy, and hot water is especially hard on clothes, sucking color from fabrics faster. Look for eco-friendly detergents (to avoid those phosphates!) that are made especially for cold-water wash.
- Set up a drying rack next to your dryer, and hang dainties, socks, and polyester (including quick-dry athletic clothes and polar fleece). What you do put in the dryer will dry that much faster without all the extra volume.

- Consider line drying your clothes outside, at least when the weather's nice. The sun and breezes will dry your clothes for free, and you'll get a bit of a workout bringing the clothes outside and then back in. As a bonus, the sun's UV rays work as a natural antibacterial agent, due to the fact that UV rays kill bacteria.

- Stop using chlorine bleaches and fabric softeners. Both are toxic to the environment; if you need to use bleach on stains, use it sparingly, and choose an

Green Shopping Basket

Laundry Detergents: Seventh Generation (*http://www.seventhgeneration.com*), Next to Godliness, Trader Joe's brand (*http://www.traderjoes.com*), Mountain Green (for sensitive skin) (*http://www.mtngreen.com*), Ecos (*http://www.ecos.com*),

Eco-Friendly Whiteners and Spot Removers: Naturally Yours (*http://www.naturallyyours.com*), Seventh Generation (*http://www.seventhgeneration.com*),

Fabric Softener: Ecover (*http://www.ecover.com*), Seventh Generation (*http://www.seventhgeneration.com*)

eco-friendly whitener and brightener when you would normally add chlorine bleach to the water. Fabric softeners contain so many chemicals that they actually contribute to air pollution in urban and suburban areas. Fabric softener fumes from dryers exacerbate asthma and other respiratory conditions. Try using an all-natural fabric softener or going without; I've never used these products, and my clothes and towels always seem soft to me!

Light Up Your Life (for Less)

If you haven't heard about using compact fluorescent light-bulbs (CFLs) instead of regular incandescents by now, you might want to check that you're not living in a box! CFLs are slightly more expensive up front but will save you tons of cash because they're so much more efficient (they use a quarter of the amount of energy to produce the same amount of brightness as traditional bulbs), and they last ten to fifteen times longer, meaning you won't have to get the ladder out on a regular basis to change those hard-to-reach bulbs. If you don't like the light that regular CFLs produce (I don't; it's too harsh and not warm enough in most situations), then make sure to look for fluorescent bulbs that are colored or coated for a warmer glow. You can also use shades and light covers to diffuse the light, making it softer. There are also bulbs that are more of a traditional bulb shape, in case you have lamps that won't accommodate the crazy configuration of many CFLs. Don't use CFLs in children's rooms; they contain mercury, which is only exposed if broken, but that's not safe for kids. Due to the mercury content, CFLs should be treated as hazardous waste and *not* tossed in the regular trash.

CFLs aren't the only light alternatives on the market, and even more efficient bulbs are in development. (Thomas Edison would be so proud!) Some other types of bulbs include halogens, which are more efficient than incandescents, but less so than CFLs. Halogens last two to three times longer than old-style bulbs. But not only are they not as efficient as fluorescents, they also get really hot when left on for long periods of time, which can create a fire hazard in those styles that are open at the top, especially in those "torchiere" lamps that everyone seemed to have in college. In fact, they have created fatal dorm fires, and many schools have outlawed them, so be careful!

Light-emitting diodes (LEDs) are super-efficient, using just 2 to 3 watts of power for a bright light. If you've seen those cool outdoor path lights that run on solar energy, they probably use this type of bulb. Computer screens and some TV screens also use them. They don't take much energy to create light because they produce almost no heat to do so. There are now LED bulbs available, and though they are a bit pricey, their cost will come down as more people buy them. Lamps with labels like "environmentally friendly" often came with this kind of bulb.

When thinking about lighting up your space, make it a priority to switch inefficient bulbs with efficient ones like CFLs or LEDs in the places where your lights are on the most first. If your kitchen dome is on whenever it's dark out (or even when it's not), switch that bulb before you bother with the basement light that you use twice a week when doing laundry. Also, don't forget to take advantage of natural light, opening your curtains and blinds when you need to see, and sitting outside when it's nice instead of indoors under a lamp. Motion sensors, which only go on when you're in a room, are a great option if you always forget to turn off the lights!

Green Shopping Basket

 LED and CFL Bulbs: 1000 Bulbs (*http://www .1000bulbs.com*), Let's Go Green Eco-Friendly Products (*http://www.letsgogreen.biz*), Lowe's (*http://www.lowes.com*), Sylvania (*http://www.sylvania.com/ ConsumerProducts/LightingForHome/Products/Fluorescent/*)

EIGHT EASY WAYS TO SAVE ENERGY AROUND THE HOUSE

1. Turn down the temperature on your water heater; most water heaters are keeping water hotter than

you really need all day and night long. They are commonly set at 140 degrees; you can comfortably lower that to 120 degrees. (I keep mine at around 115, and that does the trick for a three-person household.) Turn yours down and it's likely you won't notice a difference in the availability or amount of hot water, but you will save money.

2. On the sunny side of your house, close your blinds in the summer, and open them in the winter during the day. This will keep your house from heating up on warm days, saving on AC costs, and during cooler months will welcome free solar energy to help heat your space.

3. Turn your heat up or down 2 degrees; it may not sound like much, but a 2-degree change means you can knock 6 percent off your heating bill. Many people keep their homes heated at 70 degrees or higher; see how low you can go and still be comfortable. (I find 65 just fine, but it's really up to you.) In the winter, wear an extra layer and keep your feet covered and you'll be comfortable turning the thermostat down. If you spend a lot of time in one room, you can also use a space heater to keep that room a bit warmer, instead of heating the whole house. In the summer, use fans to move air around instead of cranking the AC. Moving air will make it seem several degrees cooler than it is.

4. A programmable thermostat is a small investment that will save you serious cash. By setting the heat and AC to automatically rise when you're home and fall when you're asleep, away, or at work, you'll never wake up to a cold house in the winter, or a sweltering house in the summer.

5. Especially if you live in an older house, spending an hour in the autumn covering your windows with layers of clear plastic (so you will still get light) can really pay off because it insulates the house much more securely. If you have storm windows and doors, don't let laziness keep you from installing them. You'll keep annoying drafts out of your house to boot!

6. Installing an attic exhaust fan is another inexpensive investment that will save you money and keep you cooler (especially if your house doesn't have AC). If you are venting the hot air out of the house, it will naturally force cooler air into your living areas.

7. Some people are still saying (erroneously) that turning off your computer and turning it on again takes more energy than leaving it on. This is not true for newer computers (like those made since 1995), so shutting off the CPU and the monitor when you're not using it for more than thirty minutes is a smart thing to do.

8. An empty fridge isn't as efficient as a full one, since food and beverages act as insulators, keeping it colder. Keeping your fridge stocked will keep you from eating out as much, saving you money (and probably your waistline as well!).

Chickie Tip: Research Those Rebates!

If you make energy efficiency upgrades to your house, you probably qualify for a tax credit under the Energy Policy Act of 2005. Tax credits are better than deductions, since you get the money directly credited to you on your tax form. This means you get more money back or a lower tax bill right off the bat. Improvements to windows, exterior doors, skylights, insulation, heating equipment (like furnaces), and water heaters can all qualify if they're more efficient than what you have now. Up to 10 percent of your cost (not including installation) counts.

Your state may also be jumping on the energy efficiency bandwagon, and you might be able to get a rebate from them that will cover part or all of the cost differential between an efficient appliance and a super-efficient one, leaving you with fewer up-front costs and lower electricity bills for years to come.

The database of State Incentives for Renewables & Efficiency can help you sort out what is available in your state at *http://www.dsireusa.org/*. You can also check with your state's tax office. You should be able to find contact information for

them online, or you can call your state capital's
line. Ask about what programs they might have for .
this area; some states will probably have their own specific
Web pages or publications to explain local programs.

Choose Renewable Electricity

Even if you don't have the space or money to install a solar
array or wind farm where you live, you can run your home on
these kinds of alternative energies. For about $3 to $5 a
month, you can sign up for renewable electricity through your
current utility provider. While not every single utility has
these options available, many do, and more are jumping on
the bandwagon every day. This program is available through
most local utility companies, and nothing changes about how
you get or use your electricity, because it's still coming to
you from the megalithic-sounding Grid. How it works is this:
by paying a small premium (if you've done even a few of the
energy-saving tips above, you will have saved this much
money already anyway), you are opting to get your portion of
electricity generated by wind, solar, biogas, or small hydropower. It is fed into the Grid, and you take energy from the
Grid. So even though you are not directly using a solar panel
or other form of alternative energy generation, you are supporting the growth of these forms of energy. They need all the
support they can get; as soon as a customer base is solidified

for these technologies, the more comfortable investors will be building more of them.

If you don't take advantage of your utilities' renewable power option, your electricity is coming from a nuclear, coal, or oil-fired power plant. Nukes don't contribute to global warming, but mining for uranium is incredibly destructive, and we still haven't figured out what to do with nuclear waste. Coal and oil plants contribute to global warming, acid rain, and particulate pollution (that's the stuff that hangs in the air locally and causes respiratory problems), so your support of alternative electricity now and in the future will mean less dependence on foreign oil, cleaner air, and less nuclear waste rotting away in the ground for the next ten thousand years. Signing up for renewable energy is something that both home-owners and renters can do. (If you live at home and help pay your family's utility bills, you have a vested interest to suggest switching over.) Contact your utility company and ask about this kind of program, or go to the U.S. Department of Energy Green Power Network home page at *http://www.eere.energy. gov/greenpower/*. You will see a clickable map, which you can use to search for local providers of renewable electricity, and in some cases you will even have a choice about what kind of generation you're interested in, whether it be solar, biogas, small hydro, wind, or another kind.

Alternative Energy Sources: What Do the Buzzwords Really Mean?

SOLAR. The sun supports nearly all life on Earth, and with new (and rapidly evolving) technologies, it is becoming a legit way to generate electricity too. Solar energy makes power one of two ways: either heating water and using that heat to create electricity (like a steam engine), or through the photovoltaic effect, where solar energy can be converted to electricity when photons hit a semiconducting material (silicon is the most common) and negatively charged electrons fly off, which produces an electric current (solar panels use this technology). Not only are huge solar arrays being set up to generate power on a large scale, but governments, businesses, and homeowners are also getting in on the action, and you can even find solar panels that are integrated into roof tiles so you wouldn't even know who's "off-Grid" and who's not!

BIOGAS. Biodegradable wastes, like manure, sewage sludge, garden and food wastes all decompose (anaerobically) and give off gases, which can be used for combustion and electricity generation. Air pollution is minimal, and the whole process is carbon neutral.

SMALL HYDRO. Large hydropower (read: dams) projects are notoriously fraught with environmental problems, the most famous of which, the Three Gorges Dam in China, not only displaced people and wildlife from their homelands but also wreaked havoc on and destroyed ecosystems. Small hydropower projects use the same idea—harnessing energy from water moving downgrade—to generate electricity. Because of their smaller size and lack of (or minimal) reservoirs, they allow fish and other animals to migrate upstream, and they don't significantly disturb the environment. Micro hydro systems are those that are so small they only produce enough electricity to power a home or small business.

WIND. Wind has long been used to create power (think of Dutch windmills, which were used to grind grains), and some countries, like Spain, Germany, and Denmark use it for a significant portion of their countries' electricity generation. Wind turbines generate electricity, whereas windmills directly convert wind energy into mechanical movement, so they are a bit different. The only drawback to wind power is that air movement can be variable, so new turbine sites are carefully considered to make sure they are in pretty windy places. Interestingly, wind power is technically really solar power, since wind is caused by uneven heating of the Earth's surface by the sun.

ECO QUICKIE.

 Wind power generation quadrupled from 2000 to 2006, and it accounts for 1 percent of the world's power.

Seven

Feed Yourself from the Earth (Not from a Box)

The benefit of making food choices that are good for the planet is that in almost every case, they're better choices for your health too. Whether you are living in a big city with a tiny kitchen, still at home with your parents, eating food cooked on a hot plate in your college dorm, or sharing a kitchen with a few roommates, there are simple, delicious ways to eat both well and planet-friendly.

How to Eat Organic (Without Going Broke)

One of the arguments that I often hear against organic foods is how much more expensive they are. The good news is that as they increase in popularity (and they are more and more sought after all the time), the prices for organic produce and packaged foods go down. So the more of us that buy them, the cheaper they get! At the closest large grocery store to my home, I can often find organic apples, tomatoes, and lettuce (especially when it's in season) for just a bit more, or the same price as conventional fruits and veggies. Keep your eye out for sales and specials on organics, and use the list on page 139 to make the best organic choices so you won't break the bank.

Why Organic Really, Really Matters

Sometimes there's no way around it. You will pay more for organic produce, but it's not because it's hip or trendy; it's because it costs a little more to grow and pick. Americans spend a smaller proportion of their income on their food than people in most other countries, and there's a reason our food comes so cheap. Loading crops up with chemicals from pesticides to herbicides to fertilizers means more of it can be grown on smaller areas of land, which means cheaper prices. But who pays when nutrient-rich topsoil, which can take hundreds of years to build up, is depleted and blows away in the wind? Who pays when chemicals used on farmers' fields poison songbirds? Who's responsible when the Mississippi River is polluted with artificial fertilizers from midwestern farms, creating a 20,000-square-mile oxygen-deprived area in the Gulf of Mexico called the Dead Zone because nothing can live there? The truth is that we all pay when our tax dollars go to clean up these messes, or another acre of land becomes a desert, and the birds and fish pay with their lives. Even the farmer pays, possibly with his or her health or fertility, both of which are linked to increased use of chemicals on farms. Who doesn't pay? The company that made money selling the chemical.

Keep in mind when you are at the supermarket debating spending fifty cents more for organic produce that not only will it taste better (high-end restaurant chefs have been choosing organic produce for years before it was trendy for this very reason) but it's also better for you. A recent European Union study found that organic veggies have 40 percent more antioxidants, which are believed to prevent cancer, and flavonoids, which are thought to prevent heart disease. Organic milk was found to have 90 percent more antioxidants than conventional moo juice. So consider the extra expense an investment in your health and the health of farming communities by keeping harmful chemicals out of your body.

Say No to Globe-Trotting Food: Go Local!

The downside of organics is that they suffer from some of the same problems that conventional foods do, most significantly, that they travel much too far to get to your plate. Up until just about seventy-five years ago, everyone ate local foods because they didn't have much of a choice! Today you can go to the market and find tropical fruit from Hawaii or Tahiti in the middle of the winter, and most vegetables are available year-round. There are eggs from three states away and "fresh" salsa made 350 miles away. These distances are true for organics as well. Our food travels an average of 1,500 to 3,000 miles from where it grows to our neighborhood grocery store. Just think of the amount of energy shipping this food across the planet uses, and that's not even counting the power needed to manufacture processed foods, or what's needed to refrigerate and cook it. By the time food is packaged and shipped, we're spending more money and fossil fuels—total energy—than we get from the food by eating it. What a waste! So, if you have the choice, eat local! Or as locally as you can.

ECO QUICKIE.

Our food production system is a big energy waster; it takes ten to fifteen calories' worth of fossil fuel energy to create one calorie of food! That's 1,500 liters of oil per person to grow food!

It's All About the Seasons: How to Shop the Farmers' Market and What to Do with All Your Goodies

If you've never shopped at a farmers' market, you're in for a treat. (To find the market nearest to you, the U.S. Department of Agriculture has a handy-dandy map that will show you where they are in your state at: *http://www.ams.usda .gov/farmersmarkets/map.htm*).

Farmers' market food is (of course!) fresh from local fields, and most markets have more than just fruits and veggies. My local markets offer artisan cheeses; yogurts made from goat's milk, sheep's milk, and cow's milk; just-baked breads and pastries; fresh fruit pies; cut in-season flowers; herbs (both cut and in pots so you can grow them at home); local honey; organic poultry, fish, beef, and more, depending on the season. In the spring some markets offer compost, fertilizers, and starter garden plants, and in the autumn you'll find pumpkins and gourds of curious sizes and shapes, and dried corn in gorgeous hues to use for Halloween and Thanksgiving decorations.

If you don't know, or have forgotten what time of year different fruits and veggies are ready to be devoured in your area, regular trips to the farmers' market will get you back into the natural rhythms of your part of the world. This is also a great tactic for learning about a new city or town in a part of the country you've never lived before. As a bonus, most farmers selling their treats at a market will be able to answer all the burning questions you may have about produce, and they will often be able to provide great recipe ideas. Don't be afraid to ask what something is if you don't recognize it. Just ask, "So, what can I do with this thing?"

Most farmers' markets in northern areas run from May to September but many go later (sometimes until just before Christmas). In California and the South, where the growing season is longer than near my New England home, they can go all year-round! (I'm jealous!)

Not only can you find produce at the farmers' market that you would never find at the supermarket (like tatsoi, a relative of bok choi, flying saucer summer squash, or blossoms for stuffing and frying), you're directly supporting local farmers.

Simple But Important: Reasons to Buy from Local Farmers

⊙ Buying from farms near where you live means that farmed land will stay agricultural, instead of being turned into yet another housing development or golf course.

⊙ Eating local foods keeps you in touch with the seasons, your region's cuisine, and local specialties.

⊙ The closer your food is grown to where you eat it, the less energy it takes to get to you, meaning less

CO_2 in the atmosphere, and less contribution to global warming!

⊙ Locally grown food, if not organic, normally means fewer pesticides, since food doesn't have to "survive" transportation over many miles. (And this means fewer or no preservatives for processed foods like salsas, breads, and jams.)

⊙ Fresh foods taste better, and research has shown that the fresher the produce, the more vitamins and minerals it retains. It's simple. The shorter the distance food is transported, and the less it is processed, the better for you and for the Earth.

ECO QUICKIE.

Food travels 50 percent farther to get to your plate than it did even a decade ago.

It's really fun to make a complete dinner out of your farmers' market finds. These fresh foods are also a great reason to throw a small dinner party; you can prepare most of the food in advance of your guests' arrival or ask them to help wash, chop, and dress over a glass of (local?) wine in the kitchen. Below is a sample menu, just to give you an idea of how you can have a restaurant-quality meal at home. It's all veggies, but you'll be satisfied by the end of dinner, trust me!

Starter:

Arugula and Dandelion Leaves Salad with Walnuts, Pecans, or Pine Nuts

- ⊙ Toss three generous handfuls of greens, with ½ cup of nuts and your favorite vinaigrette to taste

Main Attraction:

Two-Minute Corn on the Cob

- ⊙ Bring 4 to 5 quarts of water to a boil, and drop four ears of corn in for just two minutes or less; dress with buttery spread and fresh pepper. (You can easily make two rounds of this dish if everyone likes fresh corn.)

Buffalo Tomato Slices, Basil, Goat Cheese or Mozzarella

- ⊙ Slice two large or three medium tomatoes and one hunk of cheese about the size of your fist into rounds and arrange in a circular pattern on a plate; drizzle with olive oil, balsamic vinegar, sea salt, and pepper. Top with leaves of minced fresh basil.

Pair with a loaf of fresh bread from the farmers' market, and serve with a locally produced honey, jam, or jelly.

Dessert

Mixed Berries and Fresh Mint Puree

⊙ Freeze whichever berries look freshest to you at the farmers' market for a few hours after you return. Average about one cup fresh berries per person. Feel free to mix blueberries, raspberries, strawberries, blackberries, gooseberries, and huckleberries, or choose just one. Throw them into a blender with some fresh mint, and maybe a touch of fresh local honey or agave (a natural, honeylike sweetener made from the agave plant). Blend and serve in champagne glasses, and garnish with a sprig of mint.

Breakdown: Top Ten Fruits and Veggies to Eat Organic (Even If Nothing Else Is)

Okay, so you're in a rush to get home after a long day at work, and you didn't make it to the farmers' market this week, or maybe it's the middle of winter. The produce section is brimming with a rainbow of options, some organic, some not, and you're on a budget. What are your best choices? There are three solid rules to start with:

1. Choose locally grown over organic produce if that's an option. For all the reasons cited in the previous

farmers' market section and the sections about why we should eat organic, it's better for the planet to eat local, in-season food. And by the way, the same goes for nonproduce items. Try to eat locally caught fish, regional cheeses, and wines from California, not Australia (unless you're actually Down Under)!

2. If you just have to have some bananas from Costa Rica or grapes from Chile, choose organic. Supporting organic agriculture in second- and third-world countries is especially important, since they have fewer rules about pesticide and herbicide uses (and where rules exist, they aren't enforced as much), leading to higher rates of pollution from agricultural lands.

3. Ask yourself honestly, "What do I eat the most of?" Are you a bagged greens muncher? An apples-and-carrots cruncher? Loving cucumber and tomato salads every other night? Whatever produce (and this counts for processed foods too) you eat regularly is the stuff you want to eat organically. This will have the biggest impact on reducing the pesticide and herbicide load on your own body, and on the Earth.

That being said, here's the top ten list of foods to *always* choose organic:

1. Peaches (The furry lovelies have the highest levels of pesticides of any fruit and are routinely oversprayed.)
2. Strawberries (Easy to eat without washing, and methyl bromide is a particularly toxic pesticide that's allowed on strawberries, though it has been banned on other foods.)
3. Potatoes (Not only are pesticides and herbicides used, but the soil is fumigated, killing all microbes, before most potatoes are planted.)
4. Spinach
5. Bananas (They are sprayed with benomyl, which has been linked to birth defects, and chlorpyrifos, a neurotoxin)
6. Bell peppers
7. Green beans
8. Apples
9. Pears
10. Celery

"Hot Stuff": Foodie Trends

Fortunately for us all, some of the biggest trends in restaurants (and even decent take-out joints) are planet- and people-friendly. Raw food, vegan dishes, and organic produce are becoming more and more common. But what are they exactly? In some cases it might not be clear, so don't be afraid to ask the waiter to clarify anything on the menu for you—it's a fun way to learn more about where the food on your plate is coming from! If you're a regular at a local place, let them know that you'd love to see organics and local fare on the menu; restaurants really listen to their customers.

Here are some of the designations you might see on menus and what they mean:

FREE RANGE. Usually refers to eggs or chicken that are kept in barns (some with outside access, some not) rather than cages.

GRASS FED. Beef that are fed grass instead of corn feed are healthier, as the type of fat on their bodies isn't as artery clogging. Some say grass-fed beef tastes better too, and small farms that graze their cows on grass have a lower environmental impact than factory-farmed beef. It's healthier for cows too, meaning they need less medical care (and antibiotics).

ORGANIC. Restaurants are subject to the same rules by the FDA for labeling food organic as supermarkets are, so if they say something's organic on a menu, it is labeled as such before they cook it up for you.

VEGAN. No animal products of any kind, including dairy, eggs, honey, or gelatin. A vegan diet has a much lighter footprint on the Earth than a carnivorous one, or even a vegetarian one. (See Seven Reasons to Go Vegetarian on page 143.)

VEGETARIAN. No meat, seafood, or fish is consumed or included in the ingredients listing, but milk and milk products, like cheese, eggs, and honey, are allowed. Some eggs or meat will be labeled "vegetarian feed," which means the animals that the products came from weren't fed animal by-products. Cows, sheep, and goats are naturally vegetarian animals, but conventionally raised ones are sometimes fed animal protein that has been mixed into their food, which many food activists and scientists say can spread disease among animals and to human beings. Conventionally raised chickens and turkeys are also often fed animal remains.

RAW. Raw food is usually vegan and not heated above about 120 degrees, which is just warm enough to dehydrate food but not actually cook it. While some nutritionists caution that it can be hard to get enough calories eating all raw foods, many people who ascribe to a mostly raw regimen report having more energy and clearer and more creative thinking. Be very wary of raw meat, shellfish, or dairy, which can sometimes be included in raw food menus, and if you are pregnant, trying to get pregnant, or nursing, don't eat raw animal products! The Food and Drug Administration cautions pregnant and nursing women strongly against eating raw animal products.

BIODYNAMIC. In addition to organic farming practices, biodynamic food is grown in harmony with the cycles of the moon, planets, and stars, and the soil is treated with natural mineral and vitamin supplements. You'll usually see this term associated with wine, but its applications are growing. Biodynamic farming is based on the teachings of Rudolf Steiner, an Austrian philosopher.

UNPASTEURIZED. Most milk and cheese has been pasteurized, which is when it is heated to a temperature high enough to kill bacteria. You'll usually see the unpasteurized label applied to artisan cheeses; it has a different flavor from pasteurized cheese, and lovers of raw cheese say it contains more nutrients and beneficial digestive enzymes. This is the traditional way cheese was made until widespread pasteurization became common in the early 1900s. Again, if you're nursing, pregnant, or trying to get pregnant, don't eat unpasteurized dairy products. They are not recommended for consumption by the Food and Drug Administration.

ANTIBIOTIC-FREE. Many factory-raised animals are given preventative doses of antibiotics, a practice which groups from Environmental Defense, the Centers for Disease Control, and People for the Ethical Treatment of Animals advocate against. When animals are given antibiotics they don't need, it makes bacteria more resistant to them, which results in super-strong bacteria that can't be killed by antibiotics. The problem is exacerbated when animal waste runs into rivers and streams and carries the remnants of the antibiotics into waterways, where they affect wildlife. Some meat and egg products may not be organic, but they might be antibiotic-free.

ECO QUICKIE.

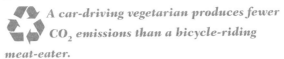 A car-driving vegetarian produces fewer CO_2 emissions than a bicycle-riding meat-eater.

Seven Reasons to Go Vegetarian, at Least Half the Time

By now you've probably heard that eating meat isn't so great for the environment or your health. As a vegetarian and part-time vegan for fifteen years (basically my whole adult life), I think it's pretty easy to do. But I've seen lots of my friends get frustrated with the process, the food, or their families while trying to do the right thing. So here's what I suggest: try going vegetarian, and if it doesn't work for you, don't just give it up completely! Instead, make a commitment that one-half or three-quarters of your meals will be veggie (and maybe some of those will be vegan, when you get used to it). That way, you still have some flexibility in your diet, so when you go out to eat, or over to your mom's house, you don't have to feel self-conscious about what you're putting in your mouth. Some people call this style of eating "flexitarian."

If all the women in America (there's around 160 million chicks) ate half as much meat, that would be like a quarter of the United States (80 million people) going vegetarian! It would definitely mean that millions fewer cows, pigs, and chickens would be bred and fed food crops that could feed people instead. There would be less water polluted with animal wastes, and fewer animals kept in inhumane conditions. One-fourth of the fossil fuels would be burned to ship the meat around the country in refrigerated trucks. And only three-fourth of the animals now bred for meat would be eaten, which would keep arteries from getting clogged and reduce the number of heart attacks. (Heart disease is the number-one killer of women in the United States.) All of this could be achieved if many of us would go full-time or even just part-time vegetarian. Every time you bite into a delicious piece of meat, think about what you're doing to your health and the planet just so you can enjoy a fleeting flavor.

Here are some facts and figures to help motivate you to eat less meat and other animal products:

1. Cow farts contribute to global warming! Seriously, cows produce methane, which they burp and fart out; pound for pound, methane is twenty times more potent a global warming gas than CO_2. And the cows aren't the only ones. According to the United Nations, raising chickens, pigs, and turkeys for food has a greater impact on global warming than all the transportation in the world. If you stop eating meat, it's even better for the planet than switching from an SUV to a hybrid car!

2. Pig farms are notorious polluters of local water resources, and animal waste from large factory farms is an issue in many farming communities in the United States and around the world. Sometimes there's just too much poop! If the volume of it all doesn't gross you out, just remember that the ex-

crement is filled with antibiotics and growth hormones, stuff you don't want dumped into a river.

3. Rain forests are still being cut down to create grazing land for cattle; according to the Smithsonian Institution, seven football fields' worth of land is bulldozed every minute to make more grazing land for meat-producing animals.

4. It takes a lot of energy to grow a pound of meat; nearly one-third of fossil fuels used in this country go to raise meat. A Johns Hopkins University study found that it takes thirty-five calories of energy to make one calorie of meat. What a waste of dwindling resources just because something tastes good.

5. Typical chicken operations cut the beaks off the birds so they can't peck one another, which sounds kinda sensible (but totally mean and painful) until you realize that chickens only attack their buddies when they're stressed; chickens are kept in cages barely big enough for them to turn around, and the cages are stacked on top of one another. That would stress me out too!

6. You'll live longer: A study in the British medical journal *Lancet* says that a veggie diet means an average of another six years having a good time on planet Earth. Don't let anyone tell you vegetarian and vegan diets are not healthy, because it's just

not true! Both nonmeat diets are recommended by mainstream groups such as the American Dietetic Association and the American Heart Association.

7. Famous vegetarians include some very smart and enlightened folks like Albert Einstein, Leo Tolstoy, Alice Walker, Jacques Cousteau, Rachel Carson, Vincent van Gogh, Doris Day, and Jane Goodall. And if you're an athlete, don't think you can't go veggie; Martina Navratilova, the tennis pro, and Carl Lewis, the famous track star, both eschewed animal products, and there are vegan Ironmen and Ironwomen, bodybuilders, rock climbers, and soccer players, to name just a few sports.

eco chick essential: be healthy, no matter what!

Remember that just because you're eating vegetarian doesn't mean you're automatically eating more healthfully. Someone can have a crummy diet even if it sounds healthy, so if you decide to make the switch to vegetarianism or veganism, make sure you pick up a book or go to a comprehensive Web site on how to do it smartly and safely (and actually read through them!). The Physicians Committee for Responsible Medicine and PETA (see Resources section for Web addresses) have information, meal plans, meat-replacement suggestions and more. Don't be intimidated; these days it's easy to be a veggie! Compared to just ten years ago, there are lots more options available everywhere, from diners to high-end restaurants, from corner bodegas to supermarkets.

Good Fish, Bad Fish: Making Smart Seafood Choices

The oceans are one of the last remaining wildernesses on Earth that we take food from; human beings raise every other type of animal or plant food (except some types of mushrooms and specialty herbs) for our consumption. Because the human population continues to grow, our demand for fish and seafood rises every year, but many populations of fish are declining at the same time. Some fish populations, especially top-of-the-food-chain predators like tuna and swordfish, have decreased by 90 percent, leading researchers to doubt if they can ever recover. This is due to pressure on their habitats, changing ocean temperatures due to global warming, water pollution, dams on rivers, and overfishing.

For these reasons, I choose not to eat fish and seafood as part of a vegetarian diet. I figure the fish have enough to worry about without us coming at them with hooks and nets. But plenty of people who don't really eat meat often still eat fish and seafood, and if you do, your choices in this area are really important. Because the ocean is a natural system uncontrolled by human beings, it's especially important that we are careful about how we consume from it.

When choosing fish and seafood there are three questions to take under consideration: Is your choice healthy for you? Is it taken from a sustainable fish population? If farmed, is the fish farm environmentally friendly?

Some fish just shouldn't be eaten at all by young women. The government makes these recommendations based on the amount of mercury found in certain types of large, predatory fish. Because of our fossil-fuel-burning ways, heavy metals like mercury (which are distributed via air pollution from power plants) are found in the tissues of every animal on Earth. Large fish eat many small fish, and the heavy metals (which can cause neurological problems in fetuses and young children) accumulate in the bigger fishes' bodies. When you eat them, you're eating whatever they've stored over the years, and it then gets stored in your body too. Swordfish, king mackerel, tilefish, and shark should be completely avoided by all women of child-bearing age according to the U.S. Food and Drug Administration. Other fish to avoid or eat very sparingly because of the levels of toxins and heavy metals in their bodies include weakfish, wild striped bass, spotted sea trout, American eel, and bluefish. (To keep all this straight when you're shopping, keep a wallet-size card, printable from the Internet, from the National Audubon Society, which shows you which fish to choose and which to avoid. Go to *http:// www.audubon.org/campaign/lo/seafood/seafood_wallet.pdf*)

A number of factors determine whether or not a fishery is sustainable. Such factors include whether or not there is a sufficient population of the fish to harvest from, how the fish are caught (in trawling, for example, some fish are caught by trapping them in nets that drag along the bottom of the ocean, destroying the ecosystem there), and how much bycatch is typical when the fish are hauled in. Bycatch refers to any fish, dolphins, sharks, eels, rays, sea turtles, and seabirds that are caught while netting other species. In the United States, there are strict rules about how much bycatch is allowed, and turtle exclusion devices are used so that endangered sea turtles are not caught. Buying U.S.-caught fish is one basic way to ensure that your fish is more ocean-friendly. Fisheries in other countries may or may not have rules regulating trawling, bycatch, or fishing quotas to maintain healthy populations.

Fish farming may seem to be a logical alternative to decimating the oceans' natural populations, but the environmental impact of the farms may be significant or benign, depending on the type of fish or seafood and the local regulations governing them. For instance, shrimp cultivation in countries outside the United States is often highly polluting of near-shore ecosystems (avoid trawl-caught or farmed shrimp from outside the United States). Farmed salmon—from anywhere—is also best to avoid, since there have been problems with the farmed salmon's diseases affecting wild salmon populations. It takes three pounds of fish to produce one pound of farmed salmon, so it's also a pretty inefficient way to produce protein. Look for Alaskan wild salmon, or Pacific wild salmon, which have the healthiest populations.

How to know where your fish comes from? At a restaurant, you will have to ask, and the chef may or may not know. At the supermarket, the COOL (country of origin labeling) law requires sellers to list where their fish is from and how it was caught.

There are great resources online (see Resources section) for learning more about sustainable fisheries, and for finding out which of the varieties of fish you can eat, which you should reconsider, and which you should avoid. (These designations change over time as fish populations recover or decline.) The fish, dolphins, sea turtles, eels, seabirds, and shrimp will thank you.

? *Not So Stupid Question #4*

Not everything from a box can be bad for you! What should I choose when I do want or need packaged food?

Most of us don't have the time or energy to make all our own food from scratch. When you are standing in front of a display of all-natural, organic, artisan cheese and macaroni (just add soy milk and butter!), it's hard to turn away, especially when it's on sale and you're on a budget.

Of course there's room in a balanced diet for premade food, like cereals, potato chips, and salad dressing. And there are certain things you can't really make, like coffee, tea, sugar, and soy milk. When you do buy these foods, go for quality; look for organic (many supermarkets have whole "natural foods" sections) at your local grocery and think about stopping by a local health food store for stuff like cereal, crackers, bread, and other things you can't (or don't want to) make yourself.

When you do have a hankering that won't be quiet, consider buying smaller packages; sometimes you can give in to a craving without going whole hog with an entire bag of chips. In the end, you are satisfied, and you haven't blown your diet and have contributed only marginally to the energy-wasting corporate food culture.

If organic packaged foods aren't easy to get where you live, go online and order in bulk to save on the cost and environmental consequences of shipping. Again, buy the packaged foods that you eat the most of in organic versions; things you eat only once a month or so aren't as important to worry about.

Eight

Fab, Eco-friendly Fiestas

Throwing parties is a great way to try out new creative ideas, as well as see all your nearest and dearest friends (or make new ones!). Unfortunately, even the simplest get-togethers tend to be inherently wasteful. But they don't have to be; with a little smart planning, and through a bit of guest education, you can throw a fiesta, big or small, that doesn't result in bags full of garbage, wasted food, or plastic cups littering your living room.

Quiz—What's Your Party Style?

Figuring out what kind of party to throw is the first step; then, whether you prefer keggers or intimate dinner parties, there are ways to green them up. Take the quiz below to figure out your party style, and then read on to see how to make each gathering more green.

1. *What kind of invitations do you want to send for your party?*
    A. Via Evite, Facebook, or LiveJournal, or e-mail.
    B. Make up little postcards with a funny drawing and hand them out.
    C. Pretty note cards snail-mailed to each invitee.

2. *How do you live day to day?*
    A. I'm always on the run; my house looks like a tornado passed through it most of the time.
    B. I have a pretty regular schedule; house is a bit messy but kept clean.
    C. I am very organized and everything has its place; I spend time making sure my space looks and feels great.

3. *What's your idea of a great meal?*
    A. BBQ, sandwiches, or takeout; as long as it's delicious, and easy, I'll be happy.
    B. I love a casual meal at a local diner with a few friends.
    C. I'd rather save up for a while and go somewhere really nice for dinner with a group of friends and acquaintances.

4. *What's your beverage of choice?*
   A. Beer, punch, or soda are all great; a drink is even better if it's portable!
   B. Wine, a mixed drink, or a fresh lemonade or iced tea.
   C. Martinis, fresh-squeezed juice, or sparkling water.

5. *How do you like to feel the day after you've thrown a party?*
   A. If I'm not tired and hungover, it couldn't have been very fun.
   B. The next day is perfect if there's not too much cleanup and I have some fun pictures to put online.
   C. People are calling to tell me how amazing the food and flowers were, and that's when I'll feel successful.

Mostly As: You're a Cheap and Chill kind of party girl. (See below for ideas on how to make your party more green.)

Mostly Bs: You're an Intimate and Interesting kind of party girl. (See below for ideas on how to make your party more green.)

Mostly Cs: You're a Formal and Fabulous kind of party girl. (See below for ideas on how to make your party more green.)

Parties for Girls of All Stripes

Cheap and Chill

You might or might not have a keg, but your parties are all about having a good time, with lots of junk food, drinks, and treats for your guests. You want to hang out and have a great time and do something simple and fun, with minimal setup. Usually your parties generate a maximum amount of cleanup though, with plenty of plastic cups and half-eaten food.

Green It

- Stick to finger food so you don't have to provide disposable plates and utensils. Chips and dip, pretzels, veggies, and even cake can all be eaten from napkins. Make the veggies organic, and balance their extra cost by making your own dip instead of buying premade. (Yours will definitely taste better too!) You can find organic baby carrots, cukes, mushrooms, and other crudités at most large supermarkets these days.

- Invest in biodegradable plastic cups (NatureWorks and Harvestware are just two companies that make them) and reuse them after washing, or buy slightly heavier-duty plastic ones, and get everyone to put his or her name or a funny drawing on theirs. Don't the same people tend to come to all your parties?

Give them their cup back at the next fiesta and you'll create a great party atmosphere when people realize they have their own personal drink holder all ready to go. Recycline makes festive, recyclable cups, plates, and cutlery that can also be washed in the dishwasher. If you must use disposable, nonrecyclable plastic cups, at least run them through the dishwasher on the top rack so you'll get more than one use out of them.

⊙ Next to the trash can, place a large box with a sign indicating it's for recycling. Throw a bottle or can in the box so people can see what goes in there. That way you won't have to dig recyclables out of the trash the next day—or worse, leave them in the garbage because you're too grossed out to fish around for them. Most people are used to and want to recycle bottles and cans; you just need to remind them and give them a place to toss the empties.

Intimate and Interesting

You like to throw a fun party for friends and friends-of-friends. Nothing too big, with cocktails, a light dinner, dessert, and maybe some planned activities or games to get everyone socializing.

This type of party can be the most naturally Earth-friendly because you can use real plates and silverware, which can be washed. Because you have a good idea of the number of guests it's likely that you will have a specific plan for how much food to make, so you can avoid waste.

Green It

- Encourage your guests to carpool, walk, or ride their bikes to the party. In your invitation, include prizes for the people who make the extra effort to arrive in an eco-friendly fashion. Making it a game makes it more fun.

- Try to buy as many organic and/or local ingredients for your dinner as you can, and let your friends know, or ask some of them to come along to the farmers' market, food co-op, or natural foods supermarket to help you shop. Telling them that the salad and appetizer are chemical- and pesticide-free lets them know you think organic food is great and shows you care about their health, as well as your own.

- Try a new organic liquor for your cocktails; 360, Reyka, and Square One are all organic or eco-friendly vodkas; Juniper Green and Bluecoat are London Extra Dry and Philadelphia Dry Organic Gins, respectively; and 4 Copas makes an organic tequila. VeeV is an organic liquor made from antioxidant-rich acai, and the parent company works to protect the rain forest ecosystems where the acai berry is grown.

⊙ Send extra food home with guests so you aren't stuck with leftovers you can't even begin to finish, or bring them to work or school with you the next day so they don't end up being thrown away.

Formal and Fabulous

Throwing a dinner party for more than twelve people usually requires extra plates and silverware, because most of us don't have that many extra place settings just sitting around in our cabinets. There's also a need for glasses, silverware, and sometimes serving plates.

Because you like everything to look just right, you will spend extra time to make sure the table looks lovely, with place cards, decorative flower centerpieces, and matching napkins, but there are ways to do it and do right by the environment too.

Green It

⊙ In the long run, if you throw more than two or three parties over as many years, the least-expensive option for tableware is actually buying extra dishes, silverware, and glasses, and keeping them in a box in your basement, closet, or attic. You can find complete sets at Salvation Army or Goodwill, or even better, you can collect unique dishes one at a time that together create a decorative theme. (For example, gather plates that all have blue and green motifs, or have a floral motif, or are all plain, solid colors.) Silverware and glasses can also be equally eclectic; these days it's pretty trendy to have an interesting collection of different styles at one table, as long as there's a cohesive theme.

- ⊙ For very large parties, it can be worthwhile to rent dishware, silverware, and glasses from a party rental company. Usually this will include washing of the dishes, so you won't have to deal with as much cleanup, which is a nice bonus.
- ⊙ If you feel like it's appropriate, a buffet setup will inherently use less tableware than a sit-down meal.
- ⊙ The simplest and least-expensive option? Borrow whatever you need from a friend, family member, or neighbor. Be sure everything returned is squeaky clean (washed with biodegradable soap of course), and maybe you can return the favor one day.
- ⊙ Opt for organic flowers over conventional ones (which are often grown in developing countries under not-so-great conditions for the workers, and which need to be sprayed with myriad pesticides for transport). Try Organic Bouquet, make a request at your local florist's shop, or go to a natural foods store.

For Everyone: The Holiday Party

Whether it's Halloween (my personal fave), Christmas, a baby shower, Thanksgiving, a graduation celebration, or the

Fourth of July, the one thing that holiday parties have in common is that they produce more garbage than other get-togethers. Sometimes there are gifts, and almost invariably there are decorations, two areas that inspire lots of waste.

Green It

⊙ Make sure decorations are all-natural and biodegradable; use holly, extra pine branches, and red berries for Christmas rather than lots of cheesy, disposable silver garlands; use gourds, multicolored corn, and pumpkins instead of paper cutouts and plastic turkeys for Thanksgiving. Or invest in decorations you can reuse year after year. Rather than use cheap decorations that are going to break during or after the party because they're not made to last, invest in really interesting and unique items for all of your favorite holidays. You will buy fewer of them for each event, but after a few years you will have a really fun collection that you can pull out to reuse—and which will bring back festive memories—every year.

⊙ Pick one disposable item to go with the theme. You don't need pumpkin-shaped glasses, black cat napkins, AND spider-dappled plastic plates at your Halloween celebration, or baby-everything at a baby shower. Pick out some festive napkins OR funny cups, and they will result in less garbage and stand out more. Use your own glassware and take the extra time to wash it instead of creating a huge bag of garbage, or buy recyclable or biodegradable tableware and glasses.

⊙ When throwing a party where you expect to receive gifts, suggest that your guests bring gift cards, plants, or make a donation to your favorite environmental or animal charity. Or you could set up a registry at your favorite eco-store. Giving people multiple Earth-friendly options will enable them to find you something they want to give and that makes you happy. Request that gifts come unwrapped, or suggest recycled paper like newsprint, cloth, or paper bags; tell your guests that while you appreciate the thoughtfulness of wrapping, you think a healthy environment is more important than disposable paper.

Green Shopping Basket

Party Supplies: Recycline (*http://www.recycline .com*), Harvestware biodegradable cups (can be printed on) (*http://www.4imprint.com*), NatureWorks (*http://www.natureworksllc.com*).

eco chick essential: Weddings!

Throwing a wedding is one of the biggest events most of us will ever arrange. Because they have such a huge environmental footprint, if you or someone you know is getting married, it is worth spending a little time researching how to reduce the impact of the event. This is a big topic (too big to cover here!), but there are eco-wedding experts out there with some great information. Take a look at Portovert, the online green wedding experts, at *http://www.portovert.com.* You'll find tips on how to save money and still make a wedding planet-friendly, eco-advice for bridesmaids, and links for local eco-sensitive florists, caterers, and stationers.

Drink-spiration: Organic Booze?

The anchor of any great party is great drinks. While organic booze isn't cheap, it isn't more expensive than most premium alcohols, so if you normally drink Stoli, Ketel One, Tanqueray, or Jose Cuervo, you won't notice much of a price difference when you switch to organic vodka, gin, or tequila. Organic wines are easy to find these days, and you will even see the label "biodynamic" on some; see page 141 for a definition. Organic beers are becoming more and more popular and widely available as well.

Because most liquor is made from grains, buying organic keeps the pesticides and herbicides used on those crops out of your system, and out of the soil and water as well. Some people even swear that organic alcohols result in less of a hangover the next day since they are "cleaner," although I'm sure you don't drink so much to have to worry about that, right?

Green Shopping Basket

Organic and Eco-Friendly Liquor Companies: Bluecoat Gin (*http://www.bluecoatgin.com*), Juniper Green Organic London Dry Gin (*http://www.junipergreen.org*), 360 vodka (*http://www.vodka360.com*), Reyka vodka (*http://www.reykavodka.com*), 4 Copas Organic Tequila (*http://www.4copas.com*)

Organic Beer and Wine Companies: Frey Vineyards (*http:// www.freywine.com*), Peak Organic Beer (*http://www.peakbrewing.com*), Wolaver's (*http://www.wolavers.com*), Goose Island Beer Co. (*http://www.gooseisland.com*), Samuel Smith's (*http:/merchantduvin.com*), EelRiver (*http://www.climaxbeer.com*)

Online Organic Libations Retailers: Organic Wine Company (*http://www.organicwinecompany.com*), Organic Wine Company (*http://www.ecowine.com*), Organic Vintners (*http://www.organicvintners.com*), Diamond Organics (*http://www.diamondorganics.com*)

Natural Libations

Try one of these drink recipes at your next party for something a little bit different. I've divided them up among the seasons so you can take advantage of fresh, local, seasonal ingredients, and you're not contributing to produce being shipped all over the world just for your drink!

Summer

Waterberry Martini

. . . .

1½ shots of vodka
2 cups of chunked and chilled watermelon
¼ cup strawberry juice (pomegranate would be delicious too)
Juice of ¼ lime
Fresh strawberry and lime garnish

Put the vodka, watermelon, strawberry and lime juice in blender and blend until smooth. Makes one large, frothy summer cocktail (also tastes excellent with tequila instead of vodka). Garnish with lime wedge and thinly sliced strawberries.

Fall

Fizzy Harvest Mojito

. . . .

½ pureed apple (remove skin and core before pureeing)
1½ shots of sugarcane rum

Handful fresh mint

1 Tbsp. fresh lemon

1 tsp. agave

Two ice cubes

Splash club soda

Puree apple, then add rum, mint, fresh lemon, agave, and ice and blend at a low speed. Pour in a glass and top with club soda and mix gently with spoon.

Winter

Berries and Snow

1 shot of Chambord

10–12 cranberries, pureed

6 oz. California sparkling wine (organic or local)

Blend Chambord and cranberries and pour into champagne glass. Add sparkling wine and serve for a layered effect. Garnish with wooden skewer with cranberry on top, so guests can mix the drink themselves.

Spring

White Sangria

6 oz. white wine (as local as you can find, or organic)

1 oz. apricot brandy

Juice of ½ an organic orange

Ice

4–5 organic green grapes and ½ organic kiwifruit

Fresh roses, forsythia blooms, or other spring blossoms

Simply mix white wine, apricot brandy, and orange juice with plenty of ice. Toss in fruit and stir. Garnish with flowers.

Chickie Tip: Why Not Bottled Water?

Plenty of hostesses serve bottled water at gatherings, or give them away at the end of the night as folks are headed home. Others serve imported Italian waters at dinners and dinner parties. Shipping water around the world wastes fossil fuel and sometimes depletes local freshwater resources, and all those plastic and glass bottles (even if they are recycled) are a waste. Bottled water is advertised as being healthier and cleaner, but neither is necessarily true; the bottled water industry is not regulated as municipal water supplies are, and when bottled water has been tested, plenty of not-so-good stuff has been found in it. There are fewer regulations that oversee bottled water than there are for the stuff that comes out of the tap. Instead of buying into the bottled water scam, fill a pretty pitcher with filtered tap water to serve to your guests at dinner or at the end of the evening.

Nine

Gardening for Goddesses

No matter where you live, you can get in touch with the natural world by getting your hands in the Earth. There's just something about the smell of damp soil, and planting a green and growing thing in it, that brings our consciousness back to what really matters.

Giving plants as gifts is always an eco-friendly choice, because they improve indoor air quality, suck up global-warming-exacerbating CO_2, and generally make everything look prettier. They are particularly good wedding gifts and look great next to the boxes of gift-wrapped stuff you find at a typical wedding celebration.

If you've had a less-than-successful time taking care of plants, don't be afraid to try again. The guide below will help you choose houseplants that are most adaptable to your lifestyle.

Green-Thumbless?
Plant-Growing Basics

The right houseplants help make even an industrial-space-turned-"apartment" feel warmer and cozier. Studies have shown that during winter, keeping plants can reduce coughs and colds, because greenery adds humidity to the air and reduces dust. Plants also add fresh oxygen and suck toxins, like formaldehyde, benzene, and acetone out of the air, so you don't breathe them in.

There are a few plants, listed below, that are hard to kill and don't require much upkeep. You still need to water them, make sure they get at least some light, and fertilize them once in a while, but they are as low maintenance as you can get and still call them alive. All of these should be pretty easy to find at any local plant nursery or big-box hardware store. If you're feeling ambitious, you can ask friends and relatives for cuttings.

To find the plant that best suits your abilities or situation, read the following plant-tending problems and you'll find the perfect greenery for your space.

Problem: Tend to Water to Death

PLANT SOLUTION. *Spider plants* suck up more CO_2 and remove more toxins from the air than most other houseplants, and they need to be watered at least twice a week. They have long, graceful variegated leaves. *Peace lilies* are a rain forest plant, so it's hard to give them too much water. They can also tolerate a wide variety of light conditions. When they're happy their leaves are super-glossy and they will display tall, elegant white blooms.

Problem: I Can't Remember the Last Time I Watered!

PLANT SOLUTION: *Jade plants* have thick, shiny leaves with a waxy coating that retain water. (They are found growing naturally in desert environments.) They like lots of light. *Rubber plants* (also known as ficus) are also good water-storers with large leathery leaves. They can grow to ten feet tall, and though they do need a fair amount of light, they will tolerate less sun, which may make them very lanky.

Problem: I Might as Well Be a Vampire for All the Light My Place—and Plants—Get

PLANT SOLUTION. *Chinese evergreens* grow slowly but can live for decades, so they are a great investment. They prefer low light and will actually do poorly if given too much sun. *Devil's ivy* hangs down rather than growing toward the sky, so it's really pretty on top of a fridge or bookcase. It has bright green leaves and practically takes care of itself, needing little light and only moderate amounts of water. *Date palms* are slow growers, but they grow natively on the floor of tropical rain forest environments, so they can survive in very low levels of light.

Problem: Generally Plant Abusive, But I'm Ready to Try Again

PLANT SOLUTION: *Umbrella plants* are really pretty, with branches that end in collections of seven leaves. They will thrive in almost any environment, from very low to brighter light, and don't need much watering or fertilizing to do well. *Philodendrons* don't need much light or water, and some have unusually colored, very large leaves that make them stand apart from the green crowd. *Palms* of various heights and leaf sizes are easy to deal with and pump lots of extra moisture into the air.

Chickie Tip: Tag It!

To keep track of when you've watered and fertilized, tie a tag to your watering can. Each time you water, just jot down the date. If you keep the can in a visible spot, it will remind you to get those plants some *agua*, and you can just refer to your own note if you think you're watering too often or not.

A good rule of thumb for watering is that you want to keep the soil damp but not wet. If the soil dries out completely, you need to water more often. If it is always soaking wet, cut back. Make sure the pot that your plant lives in has drainage holes in the bottom (and a dish to catch water underneath) so that water can circulate a bit, as it would in a natural system. Fertilizing should happen every couple of months or so.

Composting 101

No matter whether you live in an apartment or on a hundred acres of woods, you can recycle your food waste. All compost systems rely on the same principle if you do it right: stuff rots, and then turns into soil. The good news is it's not that hard to replicate what nature does on a grand scale the world over in your very own kitchen or yard. Properly composted food is never smelly and can cut down on your trips to the garbage bin (and the inevitable overloading of our landfills). In fact, if you're consistent about it, you can compost up to one-third of your household waste, which results in a lot less going to the landfill and more going to your garden (or even your window boxes) to keep everything green.

Plus, watching your food become rich fertilizing soil is kinda like conducting your own science experiment!

Vermicomposting

Get ready for some worms! That's right, if you want to compost in your apartment, dorm, or other small space that's lacking a yard, you will need a worm composter, also called a vermicomposter. This type of composting is great for smaller spaces because it doesn't take up much room, is totally hygienic, and the final product is humus. Not the middle-eastern bean spread, but the ultimate fertilizer for your organic container gardening.

The busy earthworms, called red worms or manure worms (yes, they wiggle, but no, you don't have to touch them), will keep your composter functioning and odor free. These special guys eat up to their weight in food every day, and their excrement is the aforementioned humus. Their casts (a nicer name for poop) contain all sorts of good stuff like nitrogen, phosphorous, and potassium, meaning that it will make your garden grow. On top of all that, once your scraps are devoured by the worms, all the nasty pathogenic bacteria—the kind that can make you sick—are totally neutralized.

But there are some caveats; you can't just dump all your leftovers in a vermicomposter; fruit and vegetable scraps, eggshells, old bread, coffee grounds, shredded computer paper (no colored ink) and newspaper, and houseplant trimmings are all okay. Go light on the vegetable oils, dairy, and meat; all these things take more time for the worms to digest, so don't throw a big hunk of steak in your composter, no matter how free-range and organic it might be. Some people say small amounts of meat or bone will break down just fine, but it might take some experimenting. It isn't complicated, but you will need to read up on the subject. The whole operation needs to be kept moist, and you can make your own or buy a composter ready-to-go at a host of Web sites and garden centers. The worms are also available online or from your neighborhood plant store. Try *http://www.wormdigest.org*, *http://www.cityfarmer.com*, and *http://www.cityknowlege.com* for more information and supplies.

Outdoor Composting

Contrary to what garden supply centers and pretty home and garden catalogs will tell you, you don't need a bunch of equipment to compost your food waste in your backyard. If you want, you can just start with a pile (keep it away from the house) and a good stick for mixing. I've composted this way, and it works fine. Of course, it's a little nicer (and will freak the neighbors out less) if you have a composting container and a nice shovel next to it, but don't let a lack of materials keep you from starting. You can always put your compost pile in a pretty bin later if you want.

Living in a close-knit suburban neighborhood, I don't have to worry about animals larger than raccoons possibly marauding my compost heap, but if you live in an area with bears, you will need to consider a composter with a top that latches. When done right, compost shouldn't be smelly or attractive to animals, but we all make mistakes or get the mix wrong sometimes, so unless you want the Berenstain bears and all their friends visiting every night, definitely invest in a container.

To start your compost pile, locate it a couple of feet away from a tree trunk, the side of a house or building, or any other wooden structure like a fence (including your neighbor's house). The main ingredients for good compost are moisture, air, and organic materials.

Start with a base that will keep the bottom layer of compost off the ground a bit; you can use a shipping pallet or simply a layer of twigs, branches, and brush. Next add a layer of leaves, grass clippings, pulled weeds, or a combination of them. You can run a compost pile with just yard wastes like these, and the only trick is that you will need to turn the pile regularly (I do it when I add new materials), mixing the new stuff in with the old. Every two weeks, it's advisable to turn the whole compost heap over, mixing lower layers with upper layers.

You can also add food waste, including eggshells, fruits and veggies, coffee grounds and tea bags, and paper products like newspaper (you would need to rip it up into smaller pieces and wet it down well first), compostable food containers, wood ash (but NOT charcoal remains), and dried flowers. To keep flies and animals out of your pile, work food scraps about a foot into the top of the pile, and don't add meat or dairy products to it.

If you live in a dry area, or are having a dry season, you

may want to spray your compost with the hose for a couple minutes, as water is essential to the decomposition process. You don't need to soak it, just moisten it enough so that the bacteria can do its job of breaking the compost down. If you don't want to bother with all of this extra work, it's not a big deal, it will just take your compost longer to biodegrade.

Some people get really into composting, trying to determine the ideal ratio of ingredients with carbon and nitrogen; when done correctly, food and yard waste can turn into rich Earth very quickly, but don't feel the need to perfect your system right away. Experience and experimenting with conditions in your area will lead you to the right composting situation for your yard. And once you've gotten all that compost ready to go, you can start using it to make your garden grow!

eco chick essentials: Bulbs!

Back in the day (like the 1800s and earlier) there were thousands and thousands of different kinds of daffodils, hyacinths, lilies, and other flowers that grew from bulbs. Each was suited to a different local microclimate, and there were a zillion different color and petal variations. Today we buy our bulbs from the same big-box stores and they all look the same, no matter where you live. Check out Old House Gardens (*http://www.oldhousegardens.com/*), which works with gardeners who have preserved bulbs over time (some have been passed along for hundreds of years!) and have some of the most unusual and beautiful flowers I've ever seen. Some of the bulbs are rare, and some are even endangered. Heirloom bulbs are just as hardy as any others I've ever planted, and the customer service from Old House is top-notch. If you plant bulbs in your yard or outdoor space, be sure to choose those that are best suited to your climate. You can also force bulbs indoors for lovely blooms any time of year. Keep these heirloom bulbs going so they don't die out, and enjoy something truly different.

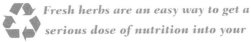
Growin' Herbs—The Top Eight to Plant

There's nothing like fresh herbs to make any meal more exciting. If you only have a bottle of tomato sauce and some dry pasta, you can flavor it up (and add vitamins and minerals) by adding some diminutive greens. Most herbs are easy to grow, and all you need is a window with some regular light. You can grow most herbs year-round, and you will save money because you won't be buying fresh herbs in the supermarket, which only last a week or so. Growing herbs on your windowsill or in your window box will also create an inviting and comfy (not to mention yummy-smelling) kitchen.

The herbs you most enjoy eating, smelling, or using for scent or oils are the obvious ones that you might choose to grow.

1. *Sweet or Italian basil.* Easy to grow and can be thrown in everything from pasta sauce to tomato and fresh mozzarella salad. For some zip, purple varieties look great tossed atop a green salad.
2. *Mint.* For mojitos and summery-tasting salads year-round.
3. *Oregano.* Try adding regular oregano to everything, from soups to flavoring up roasted squash; spicy oregano works pretty much everywhere regular oregano does, but adds a little kick.
4. *Lavender.* Pretty purple blooms, and the leaves are great for making your own oils (or just rubbing right on for a super-natural perfume). Dried lavender leaves also make great sachets that will scent your clothes and repel insects naturally.
5. *Cilantro (or coriander).* This herb is used extensively in both Mexican and Indian dishes. You'll never need to buy fresh salsa again if you keep this herb around.
6. *Lemongrass.* This tall and graceful plant is used as a flavoring in Asian dishes, but it makes a great tea too.
7. *Rosemary.* A pretty plant and an excellent addition to roasted potatoes or meat dishes.
8. *Parsley.* Naturally freshens breath on its own and adds flavor to salads and potatoes.

Pets and the Planet

There's nothing better than coming home to a cold nose and a warm paw (or four), and I'm not the only one who thinks so; the pet business is booming, to the tune of $40 billion a year. While we all obviously enjoy spoiling our furry friends, it's important to remember not to go crazy with the unnecessary stuff (Halloween costumes and bejeweled collars come to mind). Fortunately, there are lots of companies making necessities (and fun stuff too) that are good for our animals, don't create a lot of waste, and perhaps even benefit the environment, animals, or both!

Once you're sure you'd be a responsible pet companion (make certain you'd have the time for training and care, the money for vet bills, and the patience to bring another life into your space), start looking. You'll find an animal that will listen to you rant and comfort you when you cry. Just remember that pets are living beings with their own personalities, and they won't always do what you say or understand you, although they will try!

If you already own an animal, thinking about what he or she consumes is just as important as looking at your own lifestyle; make sure part of your love for your best friend with paws includes considering their impact on all the other animals and ecosystems we share with the world.

Chickie Tip: Adopting vs. Buying

Whatever you do, don't buy a dog or cat from a pet store or a breeder; there are thousands of animals literally dying for a home, and conditions at puppy mills (where most pet store pets come from) are notoriously cruel and exploitive to animals. If you want a puppy or a kitten (although adult dogs and cats need homes too!), fluffy or sleek, or even a purebred of any kind, you can find them at your local animal shelter, rescue organization, or even your local vet. Check at your local pet store too, as they often sponsor adoptions or agencies. Don't forget the ASPCA; you can check online for links to your local shelter, and you can even search national sites like *http://www.petfinder.com* for local adoptees. If you're looking for a specific breed of dog or cat, in addition to checking with your local pet shelter, there are regional rescue groups that you can contact, from Doberman to Chihuahua rescue. While there are some responsible breeders who want to find quality homes for their dogs, with so many strays available, adoption is the best way to go if you really care about animals.

Pet guardianship is not something to take lightly, but once you've determined that you have the time, money, space, and patience for a dog or cat, take your time finding the one that's right for you. By adopting a pet rather than buying, you'll be finding a companion AND saving a life.

Exotics: Pets or Wildlife?

Plenty of folks I know who love animals like to keep exotics, such as reptiles, amphibians, equatorial birds, even small mammals like kinkajous or porcupines. I understand the drive; it's fun to learn about them, watch them eat, play, and sleep. But the truth is that exotics—or nondomesticated animals—really don't belong in our living rooms. Here's a few reasons why:

1. The demand for these animals as pets means that they are often taken from their home environments in the deserts, rain forests, or other ecosystems of third-world countries. (This is especially true for tropical birds.) Even if an exotic animal you know of comes to you or a friend through responsible channels, the whole industry is buoyed by every purchase of such creatures, furthering demand. Removing yourself from the international trade in animals means fewer will be smuggled out of their homes illegally.

2. Exotics don't live well outside their home environments. The likelihood that your animal will survive on an unfamiliar diet living in a cage is low, and these animals often have myriad (expensive) health problems when they are forced to live in unfamiliar environments. These health problems can sometimes be due to diseases contracted in surroundings they're not adapted for, and sometimes can result just from the stress of being kept in isolation.

3. Wild animals belong in the wild. Use your passion and love for animals to help protect their native habitats instead of trying to create one in your living room. Check out the Resources section for some recommended organizations.

4. Exotic or wild animals can carry diseases that can get transmitted to native animals, spreading illness among wild populations.

5. Vets for exotics are few and far between and definitely not cheap.

Is Organic and/or Natural Pet Food Worth the Cost?

You would not believe the junk they put in most pet food. Maybe in the wake of the scandal involving poisoned pet food from China, folks have a slightly better idea, but that doesn't mean that the ingredient list of regular pet food has improved. Because pet food is intended for animals and not people (though I used to "share" dog food with my pup when I was a kid, didn't we all?), the government requirements surrounding the types of ingredients are pretty lax.

Conventional pet foods often contain meat by-products, including but not limited to beaks, fur, and bones. Other ingredients include filler grains, additives and preservatives, artificial colors, and whatever medications and hormones were fed to the animals that provide the meaty ingredients to the prepackaged food.

Organic, "whole foods" chow for your pooch, kitty, or small mammal will mean fewer skin and ear irritations and allergies, a lower incidence of bowel problems, more energy, and stronger immunity, which will probably all translate into lower vet bills. Yes, organic food is more expensive, but not when compared to other premium brands of pet food. Remember that when changing any pet's diet, it is always smart to keep some of their old food to mix with the new, adding more new to the old with each feeding, so their bodies (and taste buds) can get used to the new meal over a few days or a week.

Dogs can eat many different kinds of food, so going vegetarian is a viable option for them. (Most experts say not so much for cats, though I know there are people out there who disagree.) As with people, if you decide to go veggie with your dog, you'll have to make sure the pup is getting adequate nutrition. But premade veggie dog food is out there that contains all the nutrients a dog needs.

If you have a rabbit, hamster, guinea pig, or other small herbivore, try to make sure the produce he or she is eating is organic. Pesticides and herbicides build up inside these animals' bodies at a higher rate because they are so much smaller, so anything they ingest will have a more serious impact on their health. Organic pet food rules, not only because it will make your pet more healthy, but also because organic food is better for Earth (see page 130).

If you aren't into making your own pet food (see below), but you still feel like you'd rather not feed your furry friend the same dry kibble every day, you have some options. Quite a few companies make "fresh frozen" dog and cat foods, which is a compromise between making fresh food and the convenience of premade chow. Look for what seems to be tubes or frozen packets of dog food in the freezer section of better pet stores.

Making Your Own Pet Food

I grew up with my grandmother cooking stews for my family's dogs, which ranged from toy poodles up to hefty Dobermans, and at the time, I thought she was totally crazy. Nobody else I knew cooked "people" food for their pets, and I chalked it up to her eccentric ways. Years later, I know that making your own dog food makes sense from a health perspective, and it's a lot cheaper!

Like humans, dogs are omnivores, which means they can basically eat anything, but they need a balanced diet to keep healthy. Unlike cats, dogs can healthfully eat vegetarian food as well; so if you are wary about cooking piles of pork for your pup, don't feel like you have to.

PROFILE OF AN ECO CHIC

 Holistic Vet, Dr. Gloria Dodd

Dr. Gloria Dodd is a doctor of veterinary medicine who is also one of the country's pioneer practitioners of holistic animal care. She's been using alternative therapies like acupuncture, chiropractic, natural nutrition, homeopathy, and magnetic field therapy to heal sick animals and ensure long lives for healthy ones for longer than most of us have even known what holistic medicine for people is! She is cofounder of the California Holistic Veterinary Medical Association and is an international lecturer, teacher, and writer on the subject of holistic animal medicine.

If you've ever been frustrated with your traditional vet's care (I sure have) and have wondered if a more natural approach to medicine might help your troubled animal friends, read through the interview below to get a good idea of what a holistic vet does, and why. You can check out Dr. Dodd's comprehensive Web site at *http://www.holisticvetpetcare.net*.

Why holistic?

After graduating from the UC Davis School of Veterinary Medicine and keeping up my continued education in orthodox medicine for sixteen years, I began to realize something. What I had been taught (drugs and surgery) was producing a pattern in my veterinary practice (dogs, cats, and an occasional horse clientele) of progressively deteriorating health in my patients.

The majority of my drug treatments and surgical procedures were working against the body's own innate natural healing responses. For example, if I was presented with an animal with chronic vomiting and diarrhea, the treatment of choice was giving drugs to stop the vomiting and diarrhea (antiemetics, antibiotics, and fluid hydration). A few months later, this same animal would return with failed kidneys, digestion, heart or immune system [problems]. Now looking back, I realize this animal's diarrhea and vomiting was the body's way of getting rid of toxins. This had been honed over millions of years of evolutionary survival. I was slamming it shut, and the animal was becoming worse because of it.

I then made the decision to go to Europe and South America to study with holistic medical doctors. I learned the techniques they employed for natural healing in people by use of acupuncture, herbs, homeopathy, natural nutrition and supplements, pulsating electromagnetic energy, color and quartz crystal healing—the use of energy medicine. Thus began thirty-one years of research to see if these methods of natural healing would produce the same successful results in animals as they did in people. And they do!!!

What inspired you?

I was an only child born in a very small town in Nevada that did not have the services of a veterinarian. When I was five years old, my beloved dog Fanny was hit by a car and died in my arms. That day I determined I would never be helpless again. After high school graduation, my parents sent me to Northwestern University in Evanston, Illinois, where I enrolled in the School of Journalism. In high school I had many of my poems and short stories published.

But my heart was not in it. I volunteered my time for a small animal veterinarian in Evanston on the weekends. After three years of college I applied to the UC Davis School of Veterinary Medicine but was refused acceptance: At that time I was out of state, and in 1954 there were very, very few women accepted. I reapplied after taking more classes and was accepted.

What does holistic pet care mean?

The clue is in the word *holistic*, or originally known as *whole istic*. We treat the *whole* 100 percent of the animal's health issues: the physical and the bioelectromagnetic energy level, whereas medical and veterinary doctors in this country treat only 50 percent of our health—the physical only.

How do you treat animals with behavior issues?

Like any problem presented to me, I seek out the *cause. Always find the cause and remove it.* Treating anything symptomatically will never cure the problem, it only masks it. I have found many behavioral problems can be of two sources:

1. The less frequent cause is abuse and neglect. This takes much time to retrain the brain, but can be done with the use of Bach Flower Rescue Remedy plus love.
2. The more frequent cause of behavioral problems is neurotoxins. I'm talking about aggression behavior. Neurological toxins are heavy metals, including lead, mercury, and aluminum, as well as pesticides, herbicides, fungicides, PCBs, and Rabies and Canine Distemper [vaccines] (in dogs). Our planet

Earth is terribly polluted with chemicals, and there are increasing numbers of chemical toxins every day. They are in the air, the water, and the food crops. These along with the vaccines go to the brain and the nervous system. The only way to cure these animals is by cleansing with specific homeopathic products made from the offending chemicals and vaccines.

How important is nutrition in dealing with imbalances in our pets?

Very Important!!!! *We are what we eat*. Commercial diets are rife with chemical pollutants and are lacking the proper ratios and quality of animal protein (a lot is protein derived from soybean), carbs, and fats.

I recommend feeding a natural homemade diet, from as many organic sources as possible.

What about hamsters, fish, birds, and reptiles?

The same advice applies in using a homemade, fresh natural diet; veggies, fruit, and protein sources where indicated; detox; make sure the external environment is healthy. [If they do get sick], homeopathy works quite well in hamsters, fish, birds, and reptiles.

Every Puppy Poops!

The EPA says that regular plastic bags take more than a thousand years to decompose, yet we put the most biodegradable substance in the world—poop—in them, which guarantees that our dog's doings will be around for a long time too. Plastic bags are not only poop preservers, they also often work their way into the environment, becoming hazardous to wildlife and creating a mess. Look for biodegradable bags like BioBags (which are even compostable), Mutt Mitts, or the Skooperbox to put your pup's poop in. Look for these products in your local pet store, at larger supermarkets, and online.

ECO QUICKIE.

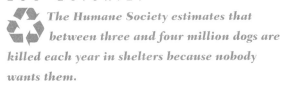 *The Humane Society estimates that between three and four million dogs are killed each year in shelters because nobody wants them.*

? *Not So Stupid Question #5*
I've heard traditional clay kitty litter is bad for the Earth; what should I choose instead?

Clay cat litter is bad for the Earth and bad for your kitty's health. Clay is often strip-mined, which is a kind of mining that removes the top layer of Earth to get to the valuable materials below, leaving millions of pounds of Earth displaced and destroying animal habitats. And every time your cat digs in the litter to do his or her business, kitty is inhaling silicon dust, a known carcinogen.

Try kitty litters made with biodegradable ingredients (which you can compost easily if you have a backyard composter) like wheat, pine pellets (a by-product from sawmills), ground corncobs, recycled newspaper pellets, and straw or other cellulose (plant-based) pellets. Some of these options are much more expensive than others; I've found pine pellets to be the cheapest and least odiferous option, rivaling the cost of clay litter and lasting a lot longer.

Earth-Friendly Accessories and Toys

Making your own toys for your animals is a great way to use up old materials from around the house. You can make a bouncing ball out of rubber bands, or a "doll" to throw, using ripped-up scraps of colorful fabric. For medium- to large-size dogs, tear strips about eight to ten inches long, and tie them together using another piece of fabric, twine, or rope. Tie them off in the middle and on each end, leaving a good two inches of fringe on each end. Dogs love tossing and chasing

Planet Dog (*http://www.planetdog.com*) offers nontoxic, cute recycled rubber (that's also recyclable) dog toys that are super-tough. A percentage of their profits also go to animal and environmental programs through their Planet Dog Foundation. Worldwise (*http://worldwise. stores.yahoo.net/*) offers pet beds made from recycled water bottles (they're cute too!).

Simply Fido (*http://www.simplyfido.com/*) makes really adorable organic cotton pet toys that are nontoxic and saliva resistant (meaning they won't get all matted looking from doggie's mouth). Purrfectplay (*http://www.purrfectplay.com/*) has lots of cat *and* dog toys, bedding, collars, and more made without dyes and all from organic and fair-trade materials.

Organic Dog and Cat Foods: Natura (*http://www.naturapet. com/*), Paul Newman's Own Organics (*http://www.newman sownorganics.com/pet/home/*), Petguard (*http://www.petguard .com/*)

Poop Bags: BioBags (*http://www.biobagusa.com/*), Mutt Mitts (*http://www.pickupmitts.com*), Skooperbox (*http://www .skooperbox.com/*)

Kitty Litter: Swheat Scoop (*http://www.swheatscoop.com/*), Feline Pine (*http://www.naturesearth.com/*), Trader Joe's house brand pine litter, Yesterday's News (*http://www.yesterdaysnews .com*) this kind of toy, and the fabric won't harm their mouths. Cats like nothing better than a few strings of twine, or even better, used ribbons tied together. Attach it to an old shoelace or a longer piece of rope and your cat will be amused for hours, especially if you drag it around the room!

There are quite a few companies that make dog and cat toys that are safe for your pets and planet-friendly. Eventually most animal toys end up in the trash, so avoiding plastic is probably a good idea and will keep possible carcinogens (check out information about phthalates in plastics on page 79) out of your animal's body. Natural rubber chew toys for dogs are preferable to PVC. Look for organic cotton and recycled toys.

part three

that crazy world out there

You may have noticed that just because you are dedicated to making Earth a beautiful place for human beings in the future, not everyone shares your enthusiasm and love for the planet. You may even interact with people on a regular basis who deride your choices, who try to convince you that your efforts are unimportant, and that what you do makes no difference. Not only should you ignore these people (because it is *only* each one of us who can create change), but as a person with a passion to do right, you also have to help convince the stragglers that being green *is* worth it. But you don't want to lecture folks (like that *ever* works!), and you don't want to get into arguments either (it'll just stress you out).

The best way to convince people that your actions are the right way to go is to be a great living example of the change you want to see in the world. They will respond. When asked, explain why you do what you do, simply and without being judgmental about their choices. Your actions, whether you campaign for an office recycling program, or pick up trash on your daily run, will encourage others to think about their impact on the world, and they'll probably feel a little guilty about the fact that they are not doing more. Combine that guilt with a judgmental comment, and you might very well cause the person you're trying to change to get angry and block everything sensible you have to say. But couple it with information and positive examples, and you have a much better chance of changing someone's mind—and actions.

Sometimes you have to take concrete actions outside the purview of your everyday habits. While it's great that you recycle and compost, what about the miles you drive in your not-so-efficient ride (that you love)? Or how about all those cigarette butts that your best friend tosses in the street? It might not seem like much, but multiply your choices by everyone in your circle of friends and family and think about the impact. Encouraging these changes in your world can be challenging, and a little scary, but think of the stakes. The chapters in Part III will show you not only how the choices outside your home and personal life can create change but will also show you how to communicate your concern and passion for making planet-friendly choices to your friends, family, coworkers, and local and national leaders, without coming across like an opinionated bore or Debby Downer.

Eleven

See the Planet—
Without Polluting It

Transportation emissions are one of the main contributors to global warming, second only to our homes in how much carbon dioxide (one of the chief global warming gases) is produced. If you've followed some of the energy-saving tips in Part II you have likely already mitigated a portion of your home's impact on global warming and air and water pollution. The next step is to look at your travel plans.

Traveling with an eco-conscience can be tough for all of us who consider ourselves globe-trotters. There's nothing more fun than hopping on a plane in the world of your own life, and debarking in another country, to experience all the sights, smells, and people you'll find there. But plane travel is also incredibly polluting, spewing gases including carbon dioxide (one ton of the stuff is produced for every four thousand miles flown), nitrogen oxides, and water vapor into the air at thirty thousand feet, which actually makes the gases' effect on global warming stronger than if those same substances were released at ground level.

Sometimes we have to fly, but there are ways to mitigate and reduce some of the damage done so that those beautiful coastlines we fly halfway around the world to see are still there the next time we want to visit, not buried under three feet of water. (There is a prediction that sea level will rise by that amount in some areas by 2100).

Driving regularly has just as much of an impact as flying, but it is one area where the individual has more control over her carbon emissions, and just a few inexpensive (or free) tips can help you save money and keep greenhouse gases out of the air. And let's not forget public transportation!

Fly, Drive, Train, or Bus? What's Really Better for the Planet?

Public transportation, not including flying (that means trains and buses) is always the best choice for the environment, whether you're traveling to the next town or the next state. Driving is the third most efficient way to go; it is still better to drive than to take a plane, especially when it comes to short distances. For long hauls, flying is really the only practical choice, and the farther you go, the more efficient it is. (It's not like you can drive or take the train from New York to Sydney anyway!)

When making your travel plans, resist the urge to hop on a plane to visit a friend a few cities away. See if a train or a bus is available instead. Though a bus or train trip might seem longer than a flight, don't forget all the time you spend getting to the airport, waiting at security (and waiting and waiting), checking your bags, and so on. For shorter trips you'll probably find that when you take door-to-door times into consideration, you'll likely spend the same amount of time traveling by train or bus as you would flying. And train and bus stations are usually more conveniently located than airports.

Try combining trips, and do whatever you can to take as few trips on planes as you can. If you are going to get on a plane, try to limit the number of flights you take, because taking off and landing uses quite a bit of fuel; direct flights are easier on you and the Earth. And when you do have to fly, consider buying carbon credits to offset your trip's emissions.

Carbon Credits: What Are They, Are They Worth It, and How Do I Use Them?

There's a lot of confusion about carbon credits, with some people purporting that they are a scam and won't help with environmental problems. These people say carbon credits just allay Western guilt about our CO_2-guzzling lives. Of course it is important to reduce one's carbon output first, but a look at carbon credits for individuals shows that they can have benefits when carbon-producing activities (like plane travel) cannot be avoided. *Note:* Carbon credits bought by individual consumers are different from credits traded among countries as part of pollution-control schemes.

For the traveling Eco Chick, carbon credits (sometimes called carbon offsetting) can be a way to "make up" for some of the carbon, which is a main contributor to global warming, that we spew into the world. There are two main plans to offset your carbon consumption: tree planting, and support of alternative energy. Here's how each works.

Tree Planting Carbon Offsets

Trees naturally sequester, or hold, carbon as part of the natural process of photosynthesis, wherein they use carbon dioxide and water and create more leaves and oxygen. Trees are known as carbon sinks, with the basic idea being that the more trees there are the more carbon dioxide gets sucked out of the air. Besides using CO_2, trees also absorb more of the sun's energy than a meadow or a snowfield does. This means that while using carbon, trees also slow global warming by absorbing solar rays rather than reflecting them. (Reflection of the sun's heat back into the atmosphere creates heat, exacerbating global warming.)

Using tree planting to offset your carbon footprint works

this way: you pay someone to plant a bunch of trees (or in some cases prevent them from being cut down in the first place, though this is less common), and the trees absorb the CO_2 you produce on your trip to Thailand, or on your cross-country road trip. Some have criticized this scheme because they say it takes years for a tree to mature, so planting seedlings won't offset the immediate effects of your CO_2 production. The type of tree and the forest in which it's planted are also considerations—tropical rain forests mitigate global warming more than northern temperate ones—but the bonus is that planting trees is cheap and easy, and can be encouraged in developing nations to counteract deforestation. It also provides wildlife habitat!

Alternative Energy Carbon Offsetting

This scheme involves supporting the cost difference between solar, wind, microhydro, and geothermal energy sources as compared to burning coal or oil to create electricity. Because alternative energy technology is still developing, it costs more than older, dirtier plants. By buying a carbon offset, you are supporting the production of those alternative energies, which results in not only less carbon in the atmosphere now but also more solar panels or geothermal setups being built, which in turn lowers the amount of carbon let into the atmosphere in the future.

If you don't already, always choose electronic ticketing, which saves the paper the ticket's printed on, as well as any envelope. Also, you can't lose your ticket this way!

Smart Girl's Guide to Cars and Fueling Up

You've probably heard plenty of gas-, car-, or engine-related buzzwords flying around, with experts trying to convince you that they have the best alternative to the internal combustion engine. The truth is, there's no simple answer to our dependence on oil, foreign or otherwise, but it's an addiction we need to deal with ASAP.

It might seem a bit complicated on the surface, but really it's not so bad, and since women decide or influence up to 85 percent of car purchases, being savvy about cars and fuels will serve you—and the planet—well.

There are two categories to think about when it comes to reduced emissions for cars: the type of engine, and the type of fuel.

Type of Engine

There are several different types of engines: hybrid, plug-in hybrid, PZEV (partial zero emission vehicle), battery-powered, and fuel cell.

HYBRID. A hybrid car has both a battery and a regular gasoline engine. They are the most popular by far of the alternative energy vehicles. For instance, 800,000 Toyota Priuses have been sold worldwide. Hybrids do not need to be plugged in and result in much better than average gas mileage by storing the energy used during braking (which is lost in conventional cars) in the battery, then using it to supplement the gasoline engine.

PLUG-IN HYBRID. This is simply a hybrid with a larger battery, which allows the car to be powered solely by electric power within a certain range (usually about fifty to sixty miles) before the gas engine kicks in. Since the majority of trips in the United States are fewer than sixty miles, plug-in hybrids can have a fuel economy of over a hundred miles per gallon, depending on the length of the trip. As the name implies, these cars *do* need to be plugged in, usually to a regular wall socket. The only plug-in hybrids on the road currently are those that particularly creative engineering types have modified from hybrids like the Prius. However, both Toyota and General Motors have announced plans for consumer models of these cars by 2010.

PZEV. Standing for partial zero emissions vehicle, the PZEV is a super-low emissions vehicle, even though it has a regular gas engine and a tailpipe. Specialized engine controls and advanced pollution-control mechanisms mean that these are seriously clean cars. One caveat: although they pollute less emission-wise, they don't have better fuel economy. Another caveat: they are only currently available in states with California emissions regulations (which are New York, Connecticut, New Jersey, Vermont, Maine, Massachusetts, Washington, and Oregon).

ELECTRIC VEHICLES (EVS). These cars are like laptops or cell phones (but use a different kind of battery technology) and run entirely on batteries; you plug them in to recharge them. They don't have conventional engines, so they are emission free. If the electricity used to charge the battery is solar, wind, or hydroelectric in origin, then the vehicle is effectively carbon neutral. If, however, the electricity used to charge the car comes from a coal- or gas-fired power plant, it isn't. But it is still cleaner than most gas-powered cars, due to the centralized nature of the power production.

FUEL CELLS. There aren't many of these vehicles on the road yet, either; the cells, which are really small-scale chemical factories that produce electricity, run on hydrogen and produce no emissions, just water vapor. In 2007 one hundred fuel cell Chevy Equinoxes were put on the road with test customers, and there are a few more other versions of these cars on the road from Toyota, Honda, and Mercedes. Right now, the technology to produce fuel cells is prohibitively expensive, and only about thirty fueling stations exist in the country. Creating hydrogen is also an energy-intensive process, but if scientists can figure out how to make the fuel with less energy, it will be a very viable way to run our cars.

Type of Fuel

The main alternatives to gasoline are ethanol and bio-diesel.

ETHANOL. Made from corn (but can be made from other kinds of plants), ethanol is currently used as a 10 percent gasoline additive in many states. Ethanol can be mixed with gas at many concentrations, which is why you'll see different designations for it. A common one is 85 percent ethanol (E85), but the higher concentrations (above 10 percent or so) of ethanol require specialized engines. Cars that use higher levels of ethanol are called flex-fuel, since they can burn either ethanol or gasoline, or a mixture of both. Critics of ethanol say it's not particularly energy saving, since it takes so much gas to grow corn in the first place, but supporters have shown that it is still more efficient than gasoline, and is also 10 to 15 percent better in terms of greenhouse gases produced. The major advantage of ethanol is that corn or other fodder for the fuel can be grown within the United States rather than importing oil from foreign countries.

BIODIESEL. There are two kinds of biodiesel, straight vegetable oil (SVO) and waste vegetable oil (WVO), and either kind can be burned in most cars with diesel engines. (Some cars do need a minor modification to run on biodiesel.)

SVO. A refined product made from vegetable crops, which can be corn, soy, switchgrass, or even algae. Usually these plants are grown expressly for the purpose of making fuel, and they have been criticized for being a part of industrial agriculture, which entails the use of pesticides, herbicides, artificial fertilizers, and of course, lots and lots of water. Some estimates show that growing plants for biodiesel takes more energy than is generated by the fuel they produce (yikes!), so researchers are looking into ways of creating biodiesel from plants that are less energy intensive or that produce more fuel per acre than current ones do.

WVO. This oil comes from deep fryers at potato plants and fast-food restaurants to the tune of eleven billion gallons a year. Because the oil has already been used once and would otherwise be discarded, it is a very Earth-friendly fuel. The best part is that when you drive around in a WVO-using car, your exhaust smells like french fries! To run on WVO, cars need some modification, a conversion handled by Massachusetts-based Greasecar and other enterprises.

Super Easy Things You Can Do to Make Your Old Clunker More Fuel Efficient

1. *Tune 'er up!* Regular oil changes and a tuned engine will make your car run as well as it can—about 4 percent more efficiently. Replacing a clogged air filter can increase your efficiency by another 10 percent, so be sure to mention that to your mechanic.

2. *Reduce your drag.* Filling tires to the right level will make your car about 3 percent more efficient. Check the owner's manual for details about how much PSI (that's pounds per square inch) your tires should have, then compare that to what the gauge at the gas station air tank says. Avoid oversize and performance tires, all of which create more drag (like underfilled tires) between the road and the surface of your tires and hence use more gas.

3. *Practice Zen driving.* Use cruise control on the highway, and accelerate and brake as evenly as you can. Sharp stopping and starting sucks up gas like there's no tomorrow—and we all want one!

4. *Idle not.* Turn the engine off if you're stopping for more than thirty seconds. After ten seconds of idling, your car has already used more fuel than it would if you shut off the engine and then started it back up again. In places with cold winters, you don't need to warm your car up for five or ten minutes; thirty seconds is good enough, since modern cars are designed for this kind of use.

5. *Streamline.* Remove roof racks, pods, and excess weight from your trunk, unless you're actually using that stuff. All of it adds weight and/or creates drag, driving down your fuel efficiency and costing you bucks you could spend on something way more fun.

eco chick essentials: Eating Good and Green on the Go!

I love a good road trip: the amazing sights, the unreproducible sounds, the funky pictures, the drama of finding a place to sleep. So fun! But the food is often just plain awful, and if you're like me and absolutely detest fast food, pick up a copy of *Healthy Highways: The Traveler's Guide to Healthy Eating*, by Nikki and David Goldbeck. Inside are maps of each state (so you can put them side by side with your road map) labeled with designations of local natural foods restaurants, supermarkets, and delis. The Goldbecks fill you in on the details of each venue, including how vegetarian- or vegan-friendly they are. Once you buy the book you have access to their constantly updated Web site (*http://www.healthyhighways.com/hh-info.shtml*) so you never need to be stuck staring at a McDonald's menu in abject horror with a rumbling tummy again.

? Not So Stupid Question #6
"May I Please Call a Cab?"

If you live in a city, the temptation to grab a cab when you're running late is huge. Taking the subway, trolley, or bus should be your go-to mode of transport; every time you ride in a car or taxi in a city, you're directly contributing to a reduction in the air quality for you and all your neighbors. Try to minimize trips in which you are the sole occupant of a taxi (besides the driver). Taking a taxi can be a relatively fuel-efficient way to travel, as long as there are at least two passengers in the car along with the driver. However, you should always call a cab if you think that walking or riding a bike would be unsafe. In some *situations, you need to catch a ride to get home safely. Think safety first, and environmental impact next.*

Eco-Travel: What's Really Important When Traveling Planet-Friendly

Seeing the world is one of life's greatest adventures, and even though moving you and your stuff around uses resources (there's no way around that), there are more Earth-friendly choices you can make when you decide you need to spend some time at the beach, in the mountains, or anywhere in between. Ecotourism has come a long way in a short time; whether you are interested in a luxe-camping-style villa in the rain forest, or are just looking for a bed-and-breakfast in Nantucket that's sensitive to the environment, you'll be able to find the place that's right for you.

E C O   Q U I C K I E .

According to the EPA, tourism is the fastest growing industry in the world.

Hot Stuff: Trends in Spas and Hotels

The newest eco trends in spas and hotels sound as luxurious as they are natural. From river-stone massages to desert hikes, spas are a great way to go when you want to get out into the natural world but aren't really the type to rough it in a tent. Hotels are competing with one another to be green, and this kind of social responsibility should be rewarded by all of us travelers. But how do you know your vacation spa is truly eco-friendly and not just trying to sell you a bill of (green) goods? Look for elements that indicate an accommodation is truly committed not only to the Earth but also to your relaxation. A truly environmentally oriented spa or hotel will have made at least some of the following commitments:

- ⊙ Mostly organic or natural oils and ingredients used in spa services, shampoos, conditioners, and body lotions.
- ⊙ Minimal environmental impact; this would include minimizing the footprint (size) of buildings, encouraging guests to use towels and sheets more than one night, recycling waste, composting, and using hybrid, battery-powered, or biodiesel transportation vehicles.
- ⊙ Landscaping with native, noninvasive species of plants.
- ⊙ Support of local land conservation projects.
- ⊙ Use of local food and resources (rather than shipping them in), and hiring local people to work at the hotel and spa.
- ⊙ Environmental education should be part of your visit; you should be learning about the unique eco-

system in which you're staying, and there should be hikes and other outdoor activities that will help you get in touch with it, with minimal impact of course.

⊙ Recycling of "gray water," which is water from sinks, showers, and rainwater caught from rooftop drains. Filtering this water and using it for landscaping (as opposed to using local freshwater resources for watering) is a popular and sensible way to deal with wastewater on a large scale, as at a hotel or spa.

⊙ Certification from the International Ecotourism Society or from a local or countrywide program. In Australia there's the Nature and Ecotourism Accreditation Program, and in Costa Rica there's the Certification for Sustainable Tourism, for example.

If you're serious about choosing an eco-friendly vacation lodging and travel, it's worth putting a little time into an Internet search of your desired destination and "ecotourism," "eco-friendly travel" or "ecotravel," and determining what exact steps your accommodation is taking. Most resorts that are serious about environmental responsibility have a laundry list of actions they take on behalf of the planet and are proud to detail them on their sites.

Top Seven Green Travel Tips

However you travel, you always need to take a little bit of home with you. And depending where you go, you may not be able to find your favorite things. At the same time, travel is an inherently wasteful proposition. Most activities associated with travel—eating out, staying in a hotel (or even a hostel), transportation, etc.—require energy above and beyond what is usually required for regular day-to-day living. So cutting down on your impact, while still having a great time or getting your work done, is important to keep in mind.

1. *Reduce Your Wash Load.* Many hotels have decent basic environmental policies (because it helps them save money too), and you've no doubt seen signs asking for your cooperation in saving extra towels from being washed by reusing yours. The same applies to beds; if there is an extra one in your room you won't use, make sure not to unmake it, so it's obvious it hasn't been slept in or used. This way an extra set of sheets won't be laundered.

2. *Bring Your Own Toiletries in Reusable Containers.* I know, it's really fun to take as many of the little hotel freebies as you can fit in your suitcase, especially mini shampoos and conditioners, but it's just plain wasteful. Bring your own products and try to avoid travel-size one-use containers. Instead find a set of empty bottles that you can refill and reuse. All those little containers end up in landfills, just like big ones.

3. *Don't Take Too Much Stuff.* I know how tempting it

is to bring everything you need, as well as every-thing you *might* need on vacation, but you're going to end up using extra time, money, and energy to deal with it all.

4. *Chill on the Souvenirs.* Yes, pick up something for your best friends or Mom, but don't go crazy buy-ing stuff when you're traveling. You'll just have to lug it around, and it's hard to know where that cool wooden bracelet or leather belt came from and what kinds of conditions it was created under if you don't speak the language that well. Definitely don't take things from the environment; leave shells, flowers, and coral on the beach, in the for-est, or in the water where they belong.

5. *Take Public Transportation.* It can be tempting to take taxis everywhere or rent a car when you're on vacation, but a great way to get to see local life, and really get the inside look at cities or towns, includes taking the local bus, light rail, bike, or even pedicab. It might take more time than you're used to, but chances are if you're outside the United States the rhythms of life are a little slower, and traveling around town the way locals do can be a great way to really understand how the culture you're visiting works on a day-to-day level. And of course walking is one of the best ways to really get to know a city; whenever I go somewhere I spend most of my time

on my feet, checking the area out from a local's perspective.

6. *Don't Try to See Everything.* You won't ever be able to see all that you want to see of a country unless you live there, and speeding around in cabs or renting a car is just spewing more CO_2 into the air. If you must, rent a car for just part of your time away, and try to concentrate your visit in two or three places that you see well, instead of seeing everything go by in a flash. You will remember more and have a lighter impact on the Earth.

7. *Ride a Bike!* Many European countries offer bike rentals very inexpensively, and some cities even have free bikes! Take advantage of a bike to see larger areas faster and you'll enjoy the bonus of locals thinking you're one of them.

Green Shopping Basket

Carbon Offsetting: Carbonfund (*http://www.carbonfund.org/*), NativeEnergy (*http://www.nativeenergy.com/*), Terrapass (*http://www.terrapass.com/*), The CarbonNeutral Company (*http://www.carbonneutral.com/shop/*)

Thirteen

Spreading the Green at Work, School, or with the Family

As mentioned in Part II, most people spend the greatest part of their time in their homes, which is why having a nontoxic home environment is so important. But if you're a busy lady, you may find the above statement is not true for you. You may work long hours at a job and then go out with friends, minimizing the time you spend in your house, apartment, or dorm to the point where all you do is sleep there! Or you might travel a lot, practically live at your boyfriend's or girlfriend's place, or log in marathon hours at the computer lab at school.

Wherever you spend your time, you probably end up hanging out with your family, if only on the holidays. Once you start learning about the amazing new green world out there, it's natural that you'd want to share "going green" with your friends, coworkers, and family.

Your Work or School Environment: Toxic or Not?

There are some obvious and not-so-obvious ways to determine if your school or work environment might be toxic to your health. Take this quiz to learn more:

1. Was your school or office recently renovated (think new carpets, fresh paint, or significant new furniture) in the last year or two?
2. Do you notice a distinctive smell when you walk into your place of work, such as printing toner, a plastic odor, exhaust, or any other chemical-type smell that is different from the outside air?
3. After spending time in your office or classrooms, do you develop headaches, are your eyes burning, do you sneeze often, get a scratchy throat, or is your breathing more difficult?
4. Are the windows sealed off or unopenable at your workplace or school?
5. Do you work with potentially hazardous or toxic substances, chemicals, or compounds?
6. Is your building more than ten years old?

If you answered yes to two or more of the above questions, you are probably being exposed to higher than ideal levels of toxins. This doesn't mean you need to quit your job or stop going to school! There are some proactive steps you can take:

If your work/school space was renovated, and the windows open, try to leave them open so that fresh air can be exchanged regularly. If you can't, go outside on your breaks and lunch hours to give your body a respite from exposure to volatile organic compounds (see details about VOCs on pages 83 and 98) like benzene, styrene, toluene, and other chemicals. If you work with paints, chemicals, in a lab, or have other exposures to toxic or potentially toxic substances, make sure to follow all the rules set up by your workplace.

If your job doesn't have rules, or is lax about enforcing them, do some research on your own to find out what in your regular environment may have long-term effects on your health. If you work in a nail spa, for instance, you can go online to find out about the chemicals in the polish and remover, and what you can do to prevent yourself from inhaling them. If you spend time in your school's chemistry lab and work with substances that you know the chemical equation for, but not their toxicity to humans, find out. The Cleaner Indoor Air Campaign (*http://www.cleanerindoorair.org*) is a clearinghouse of links and resources if you need more information on the topic of workplace safety.

Remember, it's the exposures that you experience on a regular basis that will have a cumulative effect on your body and your health.

Lastly, if you are experiencing health issues from your

workplace or school, make sure to have a checkup with your doctor, and then think about what kind of action you want to take; a simple discussion with your boss about opening windows or setting up ventilation fans might solve the problem. Additional, specialized air filters are another option if you have nonopening windows or a building with a closed HVAC system (the heating, cooling, and air exchange systems). If your health is truly compromised by the environment at school or work, however, taking action now is imperative—don't wait until it's too late.

What Is "Sick Building Syndrome"?

In 1984 the World Health Organization published a report determining the cause of sick building syndrome, in which the cumulative effects of bad ventilation, VOC off-gassing, and certain building materials were found to make people who work in affected buildings sick. The main symptoms of sick building syndrome (SBS) are headache; nausea and dizziness; cough; eye, nose, and throat irritation; and up to forty or so other possible ailments. Because the causes of SBS vary, so do the effects of them.

If you or a coworker or friend have health problems that are triggered by or worsened by being at your job or school, it's probably not that you are allergic to doing your work! It might very well be something in your environment that is causing the problem. Because many buildings that are in use today were built in the 1970s and 1980s, when knowledge of indoor air quality was low, and among designers it was considered smart to seal off a building from outside air flow, they may have high levels of indoor air pollution. This is especially true of buildings that do not have windows that open, have old or malfunctioning HVAC units, or may be infested with toxic mold. Newer buildings—or even just a remodeled floor—may also cause health difficulties in some people because of the chemicals released by new furniture, paint, and carpeting.

Volatile organic compounds (VOCs) are what create the "new" smell of fresh paint, new cars, carpet, and plastic furniture once it is removed from its packaging. The Environmental Protection Agency has found that many indoor areas (including homes) have VOC concentrations ten times higher than outside air. In some cases of poor ventilation, VOCs can be a thousand times higher. (Read more about the health effects of VOCs on page 98). It's not surprising that to some people (especially those who have a compromised immune system or other illness), this kind of exposure can make them feel quite ill.

Your workplace or school might be a candidate for SBS if symptoms of SBS are experienced inside the building but are reduced once you are outside, during times spent away from the building, or are seasonally related.

Some "sick buildings" can be rehabbed; once the problems are identified, a solution can be worked on, which might include replacement of insulation, removal of mold, better ventilation, or repair of HVAC systems. Buildings that have endemic problems might need to be demolished.

How to Green Your Office

Whether your office is large and corporate, or small and intimate, unless there's already a company-wide environmental policy, it's likely that there's room for improvement. No matter the size of your office, the great thing about making changes at work is that your impact is as great as the number of people who work at the office, and if you do it right, they will likely take those ideas home and spread them to their families. So changes made right at work can have a huge ripple effect.

There are a couple of areas where making changes is easy, simple, and fairly unlikely to annoy anyone! Just remember, unless you own your own company or run your own business (and huge congratulations if you do!), before you try to make ANY changes, speak with your boss and/or office manager. Don't just wander into a busy person's office and say something like, "This place could be way greener don't you think?" or "Let's be more environmentally sensitive!"

Whatever changes you want to implement will go down much more smoothly, and have a chance at actually being effective, if you present them as a cohesive plan of some kind.

Below, find quick energy, time, and planet-savers that will give you inspiration to create change in your office.

Then, the plan of attack! Some of these changes will save money, so that's the topic you should lead with when making your suggestions to whoever has the power in your office to make them happen, since (sad but true) most people running companies will see saving money as more worthwhile than saving the environment (but you can do both!). Follow with any suggestions that will save time, and then extol the environmental benefits. This way you can possibly convince the person in charge that some of the savings from the first set of changes be used toward the second set that have only an environmental benefit.

If you structure your argument well and have the numbers to back it up, at least some of your Earth-friendly changes are likely to take place. Think about doing some calculations and coming up with specific savings in dollar amounts, maybe even on a spreadsheet. Remember, don't try to do everything at once. Suggest two or three modest changes; once those have gone into effect without great disruption, and once the benefits are obvious, a second round of more ambitious alterations can be suggested and, hopefully, implemented.

ECO QUICKIE.

Office computers use $1 billion worth of electricity every year when they're not even being used for work.

Save Money

CUT DOWN ON PAPER USE. Reuse paper for printers and copiers that has already been printed on one side. If everyone prints to a centralized printer, it's as simple as having one tray with the reused paper, and one with clean paper. If people need to print on fresh paper (usually not as often as they would print on reused), they just switch the tray they are printing from by choosing the right paper source from the word processing program's "set up" or "print details" menus. This will save on the costs of paper, which continue to rise, while still giving people the option to print on clean paper when they need to. If you can't reuse paper, make sure that people are printing double-sided copies, which is an available feature on most newer copiers and printers. If your office ends up using one-third less paper, that's one-third the cost of paper used every year that's saved.

SWITCH BULBS. Just like at home, using CFLs instead of incandescent bulbs saves money and energy. CFLs use 50 to 80 percent less energy and last ten times longer than traditional bulbs. (For more on types of bulbs, see page 119.) A typical office uses up to 30 percent of its electricity just for lighting, so switching bulbs could save serious cash.

USE SOY INK. Choose soy over traditional petroleum-based inks for your office copier and printer. They cost about the same, but less ink is used per print, so the ink lasts longer, saving money. Also they emit fewer chemicals into the air when printing, so your office air will be cleaner. If you have materials printed outside the office, ask if soy inks are available.

TURN OFF COMPUTERS. If every computer were shut off at night, every night, we would be able to shut down eight power plants and keep seven million tons of CO_2 out of the air. Contrary to popular belief, shutting computers off and turning them back on does not use more energy than leaving them on, so encourage people to put their computer on sleep mode (or just turn off the monitor) when they are going to be away from their desks, and make it an office policy to shut them off at night.

CARPOOL. Someone in the office might have to coordinate carpooling, matching people and routes together. It might not save your company money, but it will save individuals plenty and help reduce congestion for everyone. There are regional carpooling services online as well; try Googling the name of your city and "carpool." Also, give incentives to people who walk, take public transportation, or ride their bikes to work. Make sure there are bike racks available, and that there are safe ways to get to and from bus or train stops to the office. You could even try to convince your boss to let employees work four days a week for ten hours a day, instead of five eight-hour days, cutting out a whole day of transportation emissions (not to mention office costs).

BUY ENERGY STAR. When replacing any office equipment, whether a refrigerator, computer monitor, or copier, look for the Energy Star logo and try to find the unit that will use the least energy.

Save the Environment

SWITCH TO RECYCLED PAPER. For copiers and printers, make sure that you buy the paper with the highest amount of post-consumer content. Look for PCF (processed chlorine free) paper, which will have recycled content; chlorine used in paper bleaching pollutes local water supplies.

USE NONTOXIC CLEANING SUPPLIES. Traditional supplies ultimately pollute bodies of water, and they linger in the office long after cleaning is over, contributing to toxic indoor air. Use natural products, and buy in bulk to save money and packaging.

MAKE SURE RECYCLABLES ARE REALLY RECYCLED. Each person's desk should have both a regular trash can and a receptacle for recycling paper. In many offices, two bins exist, but cleaning personnel dump all of the waste into one bag, without recycling. Check to make sure paper is being collected separately from the garbage. If it's not, speak with the cleaning company and make them aware that paper (and other recyclables, like glass and aluminum) must be dealt with properly.

BRING A MUG TO WORK. Instead of paper, or even worse, plastic cups and disposable spoons, go to Goodwill or Salvation Army and pick up a collection of mugs for people in your office. You should be able to find plenty of mugs for less than a dollar apiece. Or you can ask everyone who drinks coffee regularly to bring in their own mugs from home, so each person has the responsibility for their own.

ECO QUICKIE.

Heating and cooling offices produces 40 percent of the CO_2 emissions in the United States.

When to Compromise at Work, and When Not To

Despite your best intentions, you may not be able to implement all the "green" steps above. Don't get frustrated if your boss is not interested or is wary about changing the way things are done. Change is hard for some people, and in most cases it takes time, discussions, meetings, and approval from higher-ups. Be patient and keep supplying information and enthusiasm about your project.

Don't jeopardize your job and don't push too hard all at once for all the changes you'd like to make. If your suggestions get passed over, try implementing one. Remember, you may have to compromise, so don't be hardheaded; smaller changes are better than none. Making sure that the new procedures you suggest are saving money can help with reticence from key decision-makers in your office.

No matter what, remember that making your workplace more Earth-friendly is serious business—we are not going to get out from under the climate crisis without everyone pitching in. Just do your best!

How to Talk to Your Friends and Family About Being an Eco Chick Without Freaking Them Out

So let's say your family and friends are completely on board with all your life choices (just pretend here for a minute), and they're totally excited to listen to everything you have to say about how their choices may be hurting the planet, and they're willing to change. Well good for you! You can stop reading this section now. If, however, your family is wary of your new or developing dedication to the Earth's resources (in reality, human beings' ability to live healthfully on the planet for the next hundred years and beyond), you might need some pointers on how to talk to them.

First things first: you know your family best, and you already know which members are likely to judge you rather than what you have to say; which ones are sensible listeners, and who is likely to be hardheaded at first but open to change after they've thought it over. Use this information to approach them in ways that will work for them. One tactic that never works for anyone is being confrontational or judgmental, so structure your suggestions as a discussion, a friendly banter, or a loving reminder, and you will get further.

Here are some suggestions for issues you'd like to see change, and how to approach them.

PROBLEM. Your mom loves gardening and animals but never recycles; even plastic soda bottles and aluminum cans go into the trash.

TALKING POINT. Because recycling is so common and widespread, ask your mom why she doesn't do it. If she says that it's too much of a bother, offer to set up a can with bags for recycling (and do it!), and encourage her to try it out for a week or two; once people get used to doing this kind of thing, they realize it isn't really that much trouble after all. Remind her of why she loves gardening and the beach (or whatever her favorite outdoor places are) and that by doing something as small as recycling, she can help mitigate global warming (creating new packaging uses up lots more energy than recycling old ones), which will help guarantee that her beach or gardens will be there for years to come. Ask her to do it for you, since you'll be inheriting the planet from her, and remind her that if you have kids, her choices will eventually be affecting them too.

PROBLEM. Your sister insists on driving her kids everywhere in a large, gas-guzzling vehicle and often eats in the running car, uses the drive-thru, idles outside of the dry cleaner or drugstore when she runs in for a couple of minutes, and makes unnecessary trips all over town.

TALKING POINTS. For anyone with kids, reminding them of the future that their offspring will inherit will probably have the biggest impact. By driving unnecessarily, your sister is adding to the problems that will be caused by global warming, which her children will have to deal with when they become adults, as well as adding particulate pollution and ground-level ozone to local air. Both she and her children have to breathe the result, and kids' smaller bodies are affected more by toxins than adults' are. Give her specific ideas, based on her life, of ways she can drive less, and offer to help implement them. Remind her to shut off the car engine instead of idling, suggest planning ahead so that she can drive fewer miles and still get all her errands done, and remind her of the benefits of parking the car and walking into the bank or restaurant, instead of using the drive-thru, which will save her gas and keep her moving. For the super-harried mom who isn't organized enough to implement any of the above ideas, consider taking the kids off her hands or running some errands for her. Use your bike, or take the kids to an outdoor area to play. If she's *that* busy, she obviously needs a helping hand!

PROBLEM. When you visit your grandparents, they prepare huge meals that are 90 percent premade junk food, processed meats, cheap potato chips, soda, and candy.

TALKING POINTS. Make sure your grandparents know right off the bat that you are appreciative of the fact that they put on such a spread when your family comes to visit. Express how loved and happy it makes you feel that they are so generous with their time and food. Then make a suggestion that it would be great to have a big salad instead of one of the bags of chips. Next time there's a gathering, offer to make one yourself, and then fill your grandparents in on what organic lettuce is and why it's healthier for everyone. To get them engaged in the discussion, ask them questions like "What were farms like when you were growing up?" or "Did you ever grow your own food?" Tell them what you've heard about how our meat and vegetables are raised now, and how much energy it takes to raise food. Don't try to change them all at once, but give them information and stress the health aspects of the argument to get them on your (healthier and environmentally friendlier) side.

How to Meet a Great Green Lover (or Friend)

You may not have this problem, but I've found that it's pretty tough to find friends and lovers who are like-minded when it comes to environmental issues. Here's where I've had luck (or friends of mine have).

- A local hiking club: Not all people who hike are into the environment, but many of them are, or at least appreciate the outdoors. Try the Appalachian Mountain Club on the East Coast (*http://www.amc.org*) or the Pacific Crest Trail Association on the West Coast (*http://www.pcta.org*).

- GreenDrinks (*http://www.greendrinks.org*): Green-Drinks brings environmentally minded people together in almost one hundred cities around the world.

- There's a number of online dating sites specifically geared toward environmentalists and greenies. Green Singles (*http://www.greensingles.com/*) is specifically a dating site. Zaadz (*http://www.zaadz.com*) is a social-networking site for new age and environmental folks, but meeting new people is the only way to find a date! Green Passions (*http://green-passions.com/*) is another dating-only site.

- If your city or town has a community garden, this can be a fun place to learn more about growing your own flowers and veggies, or pass along your knowledge to others. Being part of a community that is focused around growing things from the Earth naturally attracts people with a love of it.

- Volunteering at a local environmental organization, or taking part in a cleanup of a waterfront or park, can lead to many kinds of fortuitous meetings.

This book is meant to be a guide and a starting point for living fabulously green and can't possibly cover all the great eco-friendly choices out there. It is not exhaustive or complete; that's what the Internet is for!

Go to the home blog for this book, Eco Chick, at *http://www.eco-chick.com* for up-to-date news, opinion, and information by a team of young chicks who write for and about topics of interest to women. Join the community discussion about living greener, more sustainable lives, find out about more great green shopping resources, and hear about the newest products and services in your neighborhood and around the world.

Listed below are some great specialty sites that will help you learn more about topics of particular interest to you, and a few book selections that I've come across over the last few years that are true gems in their categories. Happy learning!

ONE: SUPER NATURAL YOU

Search

Environmental Working Group's Skin Deep Cosmetics Database (*http://www.cosmeticsdatabase.com*)

FDA Cosmetics Page (*http://vm.cfsan.fda.gov/~dms/cos-206.html*)

Campaign for Safe Cosmetics (*http://www.safecosmetics.org*)

Read

Drop Dead Gorgeous by Kim Erickson, 2006

Unreasonable Risk by Samuel S. Epstein, 2005

Awakening Beauty, the Dr. Hauschka Way by Susan West Kurz, 2006

TWO: ALL ABOUT ECO FASHION

Search

Organic Clothing Blog (*http://www.organicclothing.blogs.com/*)

EVO (*http://www.evo.com*)

Sustainable Cotton Project (*http://www.sustainablecotton.org*)

Read

Eco Chic: The Fashion Paradox by Sandy Black, 2008

THREE: REDUCE, REUSE, ACCESSORIZE!

Search

No Dirty Gold Campaign (*http://www.nodirtygold .com*)

Global Witness (*http://www.globalwitness.org/*)

UN's "Conflict Diamond" page (*http://www.un.org/ peace/africa/Diamond.html*)

FOUR: HOME ECO HOME

Search

Consumer Reports Eco-Labels site (*http://www .greenerchoices.org/eco-labels/*)

Green Home Guide (*http://www.greenhomeguide.com*)

National Geographic's The Green Guide (*http://www .thegreenguide.com/*)

Inhabitat (*http://www.inhabitat.com*)

Read

The Self-Sufficiency Handbook: A Complete Guide to Greener Living by Alan and Gill Bridgewater, 2007

Green Design by Buzz Poole, ed., 2006

Good Green Homes by Jennifer Roberts, 2003

The Lazy Environmentalist by Josh Dorfman, 2007

FIVE: SQUEAKY CLEAN AND TOXIN FREE

Search

The Greener Cleaner (*http://greenercleaner.blogspot.com/*)

Read

Green Clean: The Environmentally Sound Guide to Cleaning Your Home by Linda Mason Hunter and Mikki Halpin, 2005

Clean: The Humble Art of Zen-Cleansing by Michael de Jong, 2007

GreenThis! Volume One: Greening Your Cleaning by Deirdre Imus, 2007

SIX: DEFEATING POWER VAMPIRES

Search

Environmental Protection Agency's Energy Star Program (*http://www.energystar.gov*)

Environmental Defense "Make the Switch" (*http://www.environmentaldefense.org*)

Read

Home Energy Diet: How to Save Money by Making Your House Energy-Smart by Paul Scheckel, 2005

Home Energy Efficiency Quamut Guide by Starre Vartan, 2008

SEVEN: FEED YOURSELF FROM THE EARTH (NOT FROM A BOX)

Search

Learn about the benefits of a vegetarian or vegan diet at the Physicians Committee for Responsible Medicine (*http://www.pcrm.org/health/veginfo/vsk/*) and People for the Ethical Treatment of Animals (*http://www.goveg.com/*).

Find information on eco-friendly fish and seafood choices at the National Audubon Society (*http://www.seafood.audubon.org/seafood_wallet.pdf*).

Check out the excellent information compiled by the Seafood Watch site, part of the Monterey Bay Aquarium (*http://www.mbayaq.org/SeafoodWatch*), or Environmental Defense's site, Oceans Alive (*http://www.oceansalive.org/eat.cfm*), for the most updated info.

Read

The Botany of Desire: A Plant's Eye View of the World by Michael Pollan, 2001

Plenty: One Man, One Woman, and a Raucous Year of Eating Locally by J.B. MacKinnon and Alisa Smith, 2007

Skinny Bitch by Rory Freedman and Kim Barnouin, 2005

The Balanced Plate: The Essential Elements of Whole Foods and Good Health by Renee Loux, Dean Ornish, 2006

The ECO-Foods Guide: What's Good for the Earth Is Good for You!, vol. 1, by Cynthia Barstow, Frances Moore Lappe, 2002

EIGHT: FAB, ECO-FRIENDLY FIESTAS

Search

Portovert Eco-Friendly Weddings (*http://www.portovert .com/*)

Read

Simply Green: Parties by Danny Seo, 2006

NINE: GARDENING FOR GODDESSES

Search

Garden Rant Gardening Blog (*http://www.gardenrant .com/*)

Read

The Green Gardener's Guide by Joe Lampl, 2008

TEN: PETS AND THE PLANET

Search

Big Bad Woof: Essentials for the Socially Conscious Pet (*http://www.thebigbadwoof.com/*)

Great Green Pet fun products blog (*http://greatgreen pet.com/*)

You can find recipes from holistic veterinarian Dr. Dodd (see her interview starting on page 184)) on her site at *http://www.holisticvetpetcare.net/natural_ diet_1.htm* and vegetarian recipes at *http://www .ahan.org/veg_dogfood_recipe.pdf* and *http://gour metsleuth.com/dogfoodrecipes.htm#Vegetarian %20Recipes*

Read

Eco Dog by the Staff of Chronicle Books, 2008

ELEVEN: GOING GREEN ON THE GO

Search

Ecotravel (*http://www.ecotravel.com*)

Carectomy (*http://www.carectomy.com*)

Read

Forward Drive: The Race to Build Clean Cars for the Future by Jim Motavalli, 2000

Healthy Highways: The Traveler's Guide to Healthy Eating by Nikki and David Goldbeck, 2004

TWELVE: SPREADING THE GREEN AT WORK, SCHOOL, AND WITH THE FAMILY

Search

Green @ work magazine (*http://www.greenatworkmag.com/*)

Instructables: Going Green at work (*www.instructables.com/id/SBSOCV2FD72AH5B/*)

Cleaner Indoor Air Campaign (*http://www.cleanerindoorair.org*)

Read

It's Your World—If You Don't Like It, Change It: Activism for Teenagers by Mikki Halpin, 2004

ADDITIONAL GENERAL INTEREST ENVIRONMENTAL SITES

EPA (*http://www.epa.gov*)
Audubon (*http://www.audubon.org*)
E Magazine (*http://www.emagazine.com*)
Greenopia (*http://greenopia.com*)
Grist (*http://www.grist.org*)
Treehugger (*http://www.treehugger.com*)

The Daily Green (*http://www.thedailygreen.com*)
Earth 911 (*http://www.earth911.org*)
Green Guide (*http://www.thegreenguide.com*)

ADDITIONAL GENERAL INTEREST ENVIRONMENTAL BOOKS

Green Living: The E Magazine Handbook for Living Lightly on the Earth by the Editors of E Magazine, 2005

Making Kind Choices: Everyday Ways to Enhance Your Life Through Earth and Animal Friendly Living by Ingrid Newkirk, with a Foreword by Sir Paul McCartney

Choose to Reuse by Nikki and David Goldbeck, 1995

Cradle to Cradle by William McDonough and Michael Braungart, 2002

The Purplebook Green: An Eco-Friendly Online Shopping Guide by Hillary Mendelsohn and Ian Anderson, 2007

Just the Tips, Man. Protecting the Environment by Wendy Richards, 2006

Index